BRITISH AVIATION
The First Half-Century

David Willis
with Richard James Molloy and Sean Clark

KEY
Books

CONTENTS PAGE IMAGE: FAIREY SWORDFISH

Designed as a carrier-borne tactical strike and reconnaissance aircraft, the Fairey Swordfish was obsolete by the time it entered service in July 1936, yet it remained in frontline service long after its replacement – the Fairey Albacore – was available. Known as the 'Stringbag', the type sunk more than 300,000 tons of enemy shipping during World War Two, including much of the Italian fleet at Taranto in November 1940. FAA Swordfish I L7701 was coded 'K' during its time with the Torpedo Training Unit at Gosport, Hampshire, between September 1938 and June 1939. It was transferred to 820 Squadron in August 1939 for service on the aircraft carrier HMS *Ark Royal*. By July 1941, it was based at Arbroath, in Scotland, with 767 Squadron, a deck landing training unit. In addition to the Fleet Air Arm (FAA), small numbers of Swordfish also served with the Royal Air Force (RAF), notably with 119 Squadron hunting German E- and R-boats and midget submarines at the end of the war, while the Royal Canadian Air Force used others as trainers.

Published by Key Books
An imprint of Key Publishing Ltd
PO Box 100
Stamford
Lincs
PE19 1XQ

www.keypublishing.com

ISBN 978 1 80282 134 5

Typeset by SJmagic DESIGN SERVICES, India.

CONTENTS

AUTHOR'S NOTE

Shape and Form... and Colour

The first 50 years of the twentieth century was the most productive time for the British aviation industry. Its decades saw of production of the largest number of different aircraft types in the greatest numbers, swollen by the requirements of two global conflicts. The total number of aircraft rolled out in the initial 50 years greatly exceeded the output of the 70 that followed. The variety of different configurations used during the period remains unequalled.

Many fine volumes have been written on the subject. This book takes black and white images sourced from Key Publishing's archive – including the superb former *Aeroplane* collection – which has a comprehensive range of British aeroplane images from the early years onwards, and turned them into colour pictures. By selecting those taken before 1950, I thought it would be possible to create a book that would not only show the great variety of shapes and forms of the flying machines created in the United Kingdom, but also the breadth of the inventiveness of the industry from its birth to its zenith.

Not only would I be able to include some of the 'greatest aircraft of all time', but also some of the 'not so greats', and even a handful of the 'really awful '. While not pretending to be a comprehensive survey, the result is a good cross-section of the output of the British industry during its 'Golden Age', many depicted in colour for the first time ever.

The alchemy of creating the colour images from black and white originals for this volume was handled with skill by Richard Molloy and Sean Clark. They had the most difficult task in this project. While the colours of some of the more common aircraft types depicted are well known, next to no information was available for many of the more obscure types. As responsibility for finding reference material to assist Richard and Sean in their task was mine, any mistakes in the colours depicted also remains mine. Several other people also made vital contributions to this book, and I would like to thank Sue Rylance for subbing the text, and Brianne Bellio and Jonathan Jackson from Key Publishing.

David Willis
Wittering, September 2021

LEFT: BRISTOL BULLDOG II

From June 1929, the Bristol Aeroplane Co flew Type 105 Bulldog II G-AAHH as its demonstrator for the single-seat fighter. Its flying career was short, as the biplane was withdrawn from use in June 1930, although it survived until 1935 when it was scrapped at Filton, Gloucestershire. From mid-1930, Bristol produced two further Bulldog demonstrators, including Mk II G-ABBB, which became the first Mk IIA, and formed the basis of the aircraft currently displayed at the RAF Museum at Hendon in north London. In total, Bristol built 441 Bulldogs, including aircraft exported to Australia, Finland, Japan, Latvia, Siam (now Thailand), Sweden and two for evaluation by the US Navy. Two additional Bulldogs were assembled by Nakajima of Japan.

BRISTOL BOXKITE

The Bristol Biplane 'Boxkite' was a close facsimile of Anglo-French aviator and designer Henri Farman's third biplane model, the prototype, No 7, being constructed in a matter of weeks using published drawings and details of the French aeroplane. Delivered to the Bristol Flying School, Maurice Edmond was at the controls for its first flight on 30 July 1910 from Larkhill on Salisbury Plain, Wiltshire (as seen here). The aircraft proved to be one of the most successful of the pioneering types, with at least 78 produced. Its docile handling and low speed made it an ideal trainer for those enrolled at the various flying schools established by the turn of the decade and with the military services of several countries, most notably the British Army and the Admiralty, Russia and Australia. Boxkites were also used to compete for many of the prizes put up to encourage the development of flying and aeroplanes in the four years before the outbreak of war, by when the type was considered obsolete.

BRITISH AVIATION
THE FIRST HALF-CENTURY

INTRODUCTION

The first half of the 20th century witnessed great leaps forward in many fields of scientific endeavour. For aviation, it included the first flight of a heavier-than-air aeroplane and the establishment of a new industry dedicated to designing and building them. The first piloted, powered, heavy-than-air aircraft to officially fly in the British Isles was the British Army Aeroplane No 1, designed and flown by Samuel Franklin Cody. Cody was born in Davenport, Iowa. After moving to England, he tested a biplane glider in 1905 and was employed as the Royal Engineers' kiting instructor within the Army Balloon Factory at Farnborough, Hampshire. The No 1 made its milestone flight of 1,390ft (424m) on 16 October 1908 but although testing continued into 1909 – flying for more than a mile (1.6km) on 14 May – interest within the War Office quickly waned.

Flight Before Flight

It would be incorrect however to believe that British aviation began with Cody's flight, or even with the Roe I built by Alliott Verdon Roe that 'hopped' on 8 June 1908. Yorkshireman Sir George Cayley outlined the concept of the modern aeroplane in 1799, earning him the sobriquet 'the father of aviation'. His studies and experiments included the design and assembly of a piloted glider in 1853, into which a member of his staff (or possibly family) was strapped and flew approximately 500 yards across a small valley at Brompton Dale. This was the first successful flight of an aeroplane in Great Britain, but, unfortunately, the 'pilot' – variously stated to be Cayley's coachman, footman, butler or grandson – has not been conclusively identified.

Between 1895 and 1899, marine engineer and lecturer Percy Sinclair Pitcher experimented with gliders, starting with The Bat. In 1897, Pitcher formed the Wilson-Pitcher company with the aim of building the world's first combustion aero-engine, a 4hp (3kW) unit for a triplane he had designed. Pitcher died on 30 September 1899, two days after crashing in his Hawk glider. By then, his triplane had apparently been completed but was unable to fly because of a broken crankshaft in the engine. His untimely demise gave rise to one of aviation's great 'what ifs'.

Birth of an Industry

Towards the end of the first decade of the 20th century, Britain's aircraft 'industry' comprised individuals working (usually) at their own expense to build contraptions they hoped would lift them off the ground. Those that were successful found that other people wished to have aircraft built for them. During the first ten years of the century, Robert Blackburn, John William Dunne, the British and Colonial Aeroplane Company, Geoffrey de Havilland, Claude Grahame-White, Frederick Handley Page, Noel Pemberton Billing, Alliott Verdon Roe, the Short brothers, Thomas Sopwith and Vickers were among those designing and building aeroplanes.

ROYAL AIRCRAFT FACTORY FE2

Before the widespread introduction of interrupter gear, several fighting aircraft were configured with a pusher engine at the rear of a short nacelle with tailplanes mounted on booms, so that the gunner sat in the nose had an uninterrupted field of fire. Such aircraft, including the Royal Aircraft Factory FE2, helped end the 'Fokker scourge' from the second half of 1915. The first of 12 FE2as made its maiden flight on 26 January 1915, the third going to the Central Flying School for evaluation on 20 March. On 14 May 1915, 6 Squadron received the first FE2a sent to France. Replacing the Green engine of the FE2a with a Beardmore created the FE2b. The FE2b was built in large numbers (production of all versions exceeded 2,180) and served with 15 squadrons on the Western Front, although it was thoroughly outclassed by German fighters by April 1917. Royal Aircraft Factory FE2b 6944, named *Newfoundland IV*, was a presentation aircraft, funded by The Patriotic Association of Newfoundland. In return for its donation, the name stipulated by the Association passed from aircraft to aircraft. From February 1916, it was carried by FE2b 5202 of 20 Squadron, which was destroyed that April. FE2b 6944 also had a brief career as *Newfoundland IV*, as it was painted on around 26 May 1916; the aircraft was wrecked by 18 June. The name was later carried by a succession of Bristol Fighters.

159

BRISTOL M1C

Monoplane fighters were a rarity during World War One, with the Bristol M1 the most famous to serve with the Royal Flying Corps (RFC). The M1A first appeared in July 1916 and was evaluated by the Central Flying School that month, where its excellent performance was noted. It was not until October 1916 that four more prototypes were ordered as M1Bs, the first going to France in January 1917, where it was the only example of its type to be flown operationally, as Hugh Trenchard, the commander of the RFC in France, disliked monoplanes. The other three M1Bs were allocated to 111 Squadron in Palestine in September 1917. The previous month, a contract had been placed for 125 M1Cs, differing from the prototypes in that they were powered by the 110hp (82kW) Le Rhône 9J. They had transparent panels in both wing roots for better view downward and a centrally mounted Vickers machine gun. The first was delivered on 19 September 1917, and they served in small numbers with 72 Squadron in Mesopotamia and 17 and 47 (later 150) Squadrons in Macedonia. The last RAF examples were retired by 150 Squadron in September 1919. Three M1Cs, including G-EAVO, plus a M1B, were bought by the British & Colonial Aeroplane Co (Bristol) after the war. M1C G-EAVO was sold in November 1921 to Señor Juan Pombo, going to Madrid in Spain as M-AFAA.

Many of them went on to create firms that were to play an important role within the British aviation industry.

The period saw the adoption of the aeroplane as an instrument of war, and the pace of development increased during the Great War as money and manpower were allocated to develop and design machines for the Admiralty and Army. The frail machines that set off for France in August 1914 were very different to the heavy bombers entering service with the newly formed Royal Air Force (RAF) at the end of World War One in terms of performance, reliability and armament. More than 50,000 aeroplanes were built in Britain alone in just over 50 months, with general purpose designs giving way to those dedicated to a specific role.

The Roaring Twenties

Development of military aviation almost came to a halt after the war, due to the need to reduce government expenditure and the belief that there would not be a major conflict for at least ten years. Although the RAF was allowed to remain a separate military service – much to the alarm of the Admiralty and Army – it largely had to 'make do' with the aircraft designed and delivered to it in the latter years of the war. In addition to most outstanding contracts being cancelled by the government, the market for new, purpose-built civil designs in the immediate post-war period was effectively suppressed by the ready availability of large numbers of surplus military aircraft.

The 1920s are often described as aviation's 'adventuring years'. Flying combined an exotic mix of technology, escapism, adventure and glamour – and a fair degree of danger – that appealed to a generation that had witnessed the horrors of mechanised warfare in Europe and those that came of age soon after. Although still largely for the affluent, the popularity of flying clubs increased throughout the decade, providing access to the air for many of lesser means.

The decade also saw the RAF forge its own identity as a separate service with a distinctive role under the leadership of Air Chief Marshal Sir Hugh Trenchard, Chief of the Air Staff from 1919 to 1929. It offered a cheaper method of policing the colonies than garrisoning large numbers of troops overseas or calling upon the stretched resources of the Royal Navy. As the decade progressed, the importance of the RAF also grew in the British Isles as the theories of the proponents of air power began to circulate. These include the dogma 'the bomber will always get through', first outlined by Italian General Giulio Douhet, that strategic bombing would force populations to sue for peace within months and the only defence was offence. Trenchard also believed that the bomber would be the key weapon in any future conflict and, in 1925, formed Air Defence of Great Britain to provide protection for the capital against the threat. By the late 1920s, more than 500 aircraft a year were delivered to the RAF, although the service only grew by about 50 annually as older types were replaced and attrition made good.

From Peace to War

In the early years of the 1930s, British aviation recorded some notable achievements. In September 1931, Flight Lieutenant John Nelson Boothman won the Schneider Trophy seaplane race in a Supermarine S.6B, the third consecutive time the British team had prevailed, allowing the prize to be claimed outright for the country. On 3 April 1933, the Houston Mount Everest Flying Expedition, funded by Lucy, Lady Houston, became the first to fly over the highest place on the surface of the earth. Sir Douglas Douglas-Hamilton (Lord Clydesdale) and Flight Lieutenant David Fowler McIntyre in the Westland PV.6 'Houston-Wallace' and PV.3 flew in formation over the 'roof of the world' for a second time on 19 April. Between 20 and 23 October 1934, Flight Lieutenant Charles William Anderson Scott and Captain Tom Campbell Black won the MacRobertson Trophy Air Race between Britain and Australia in de Havilland DH.88 Comet *Grosvenor House*.

While these achievements – faster, higher, further – helped boost the image of the country as a leader in the air, by the middle of the 1930s, significant questions were being asked about the state of the RAF. The rise of Italian Fascism and the National Socialist German Workers' Party, both with ambitious plans for their air forces, caused alarm within official circles.

BRISTOL BRAEMAR

The Bristol Braemar was a triplane heavy bomber designed to enable the war-time Independent Air Force to bomb Berlin. Up to six 250lb (110kg) bombs could be carried internally. Bristol received a contract for three from the Air Board (the forerunner of the Air Ministry) on 11 December 1917, each aircraft being completed to a different standard. The second was the Type 25 Braemar II (C4297), which differed from the Type 24 Braemar I (C4296) by having an improved cockpit and controls and four 410hp (306kW) Liberty 12As engines in place of the 230hp (172kW) Siddeley Pumas, increasing maximum speed by 25 per cent. It first flew on 18 February 1919. On a flight to Farnborough, Hampshire, on 26 April, it was damaged in a forced landing between Milton and Steventon, Oxfordshire. After repair, it went to the Aeroplane Experimental Establishment (AEE) at Martlesham Heath, Suffolk, in June 1919 for performance tests, although these did not start until 1920 after the Braemar had sat outside during the winter. While taking off on 16 August 1921, the bomber swung and crashed into a hangar, demolishing the front of the aircraft. One of the two fatalities in the accident was Flight Lieutenant Oliver Manners Sutton, inventor of the Sutton seat harness. During its existence, the Braemar II only accumulated 11hrs 50mins in the air. The third Braemar was completed as the Pullman transport.

DE HAVILLAND DH.91 ALBATROSS

The DH.91 Albatross was one of the most aesthetically pleasing commercial transports produced by the British aircraft industry in the interwar period. Conceived in response to Specification 36/35, which outlined a transatlantic mailplane, only seven Albatrosses were built, comprising two prototypes configured as mail transports and five production aircraft for passengers, the latter with additional windows and revised flaps. The fuselage was constructed using a ply-balsa-ply sandwich, while streamlined nacelles housed de Havilland Gipsy Twelve engines. The prototype first flew on 20 May 1937, and the airliner entered service with Imperial Airways in October 1938 as the Frobisher class, flying to destinations in Europe. The fleet passed to British Overseas Airways Corporation (BOAC) when it began operations in April 1940. Both prototypes were impressed into the RAF in September 1940, serving with 271 Squadron flying between Prestwick in Scotland and Reykjavik in Iceland, but they had been written off by the end of August 1941. The first passenger aircraft, *Frobisher* (G-AFDI), was destroyed in a German attack on Whitchurch Airport outside Bristol on 20 December 1940. Two other Albatrosses were destroyed in crash landings and the final pair with BOAC were withdrawn and scrapped in September 1943.

GLOSTER GLADIATOR

The Gladiator was the last biplane fighter in frontline RAF service. A private venture prototype, the SS.37, had flown in November 1934 before it was ordered for the RAF as the Gladiator I to Specification 14/35. The 231 Gladiator Is for the service were followed by 272 Mk IIs with a slightly more powerful Bristol Mercury engine. The first of 18 frontline units in the UK – five with the Auxiliary Air Force – was 72 Squadron at Church Fenton, Yorkshire, which re-equipped in February 1937. Gladiator I K6132, the fourth production aircraft, was delivered to 72 Squadron on 22 February 1937. It had a long career, later serving with 603 Squadron until withdrawn to 24 Maintenance Unit (MU) at Ternhill, Shropshire, on 6 November 1939, and placed into storage. In April 1941, it was issued to the Ouston Station Flight, later passing to 13 Group Communications Flight. In January 1942, it went to Marshalls of Cambridge before a further period of storage. From June 1943, it was used by the Royal Aircraft Establishment (RAE) at Farnborough, Hampshire, being retired to 8 MU at Little Rissington, Gloucestershire, on 23 July 1944, where it remained until struck off charge in April 1946.

In 1934, it was decided that the size of the RAF would no longer be pegged to that of France but Germany, and plans were formulated to increase it and expand the capacity of the British aviation industry. The expansion programmes were initially hampered by a lack of funds, but, as neighbouring countries began to be incorporated into the German Reich and the prospect of war loomed ever closer, additional sums were released by the Treasury for military spending. The outcome of this largesse was the introduction into RAF service of successive generations of fighters and bombers in the second half of the 1930s. Many designs quickly became obsolete as the state-of-the-art military aircraft advanced and, as the decade drew to a close, biplanes gave way to modern monoplanes, fighter armament increased from two to eight machine guns and performance improved as more powerful engines were installed and aerodynamics refined. The better quality was matched by moves to increase quantity and, by the time war was declared on 3 September 1939, the foundations for the enormous wartime production programme were in place.

Total War

It was during World War Two – in 1944, to be exact – that the British aviation industry reached the peak of its output. With the nation configured for 'total war', production of aircraft had high priority, supported by and centrally planned by the Ministry of Aircraft Production to feed an almost insatiable appetite for combat aircraft for operations across the globe. In the early years of the war, the aim was to build as many combat aircraft as possible, with changes only introduced that gave a clear improvement in performance without disrupting the flow of aircraft from the factories. Several types that went on to play important roles in the later years of the conflict flew in 1940 or before, but development proceeded slowly because of the need to concentrate resources on existing programmes. This new generation began to enter service from around 1942 and while not all were successful – it is fair to suggest the outcome of the war would not have been altered if the Armstrong Whitworth Albemarle had been cancelled – in general,

the RAF was well served by the aircraft produced by the British aviation industry during World War Two.

It is more difficult to say the same about the Fleet Air Arm (FAA), which was somewhat neglected and equipped with less than first-class aircraft during the 1930s, while the new generation of purposely designed British carrier-borne aircraft that entered service in the second half of the war were adequate, rather than exemplary. To a large extent, this shortfall in performance was alleviated by large numbers of American naval aircraft supplied under Lend-Lease.

Slow Run Down

At the end of the war, Britain was in a perilous financial position. Although it had prevailed, the conflict highlighted the military and industrial dominance of the United States and the Soviet Union, compared to which Britain was a second-rate power. Balanced against the need to cut costs by reducing the size of the wartime armed services was the requirement to keep sufficient forces in occupied Germany, Italy and Austria and many other areas of the globe to maintain (or in many cases, restore) stability. In the Far East, many uprisings occurred in the former European colonies after Japanese forces surrendered, led by people eager to determine their own destinies before the British, Dutch or French 'colonial masters' returned. These global commitments helped slow the run-down of the RAF, while suspicion over the intentions of the Soviet Union meant there was no post-war equivalent of the 'ten year rule'.

In 1946–47, the RAF accounted for 15.5 per cent (at £255.5m) of defence expenditure, just below that of the Royal Navy (16.1 per cent) and a long way behind the Army (43.4 per cent); a quarter of the budget was allocated to central defence needs and other governmental ministries. Unlike after World War One, procurement of aircraft for the RAF and FAA continued, but at a much lower level.

It was clear that the new generation of combat aircraft would be powered by jet engines, making the large existing fleet of piston engine types obsolete, and the post-war era saw their development and introduction to service in increasing numbers.

ARMSTRONG WHITWORTH AW.41 ALBERMARLE

The Albemarle was designed as a medium bomber to Specification B.18/38, with major components that could be subcontracted to firms without previous aeronautical experience. The prototype flew on 20 March 1940, with deliveries commencing in October 1940. All production Albemarles were assembled by A W Hawkesley at Hucclecote in Gloucestershire, a subsidiary of the Gloster Aircraft Company, where these aircraft (with Hawker Typhoons in the distance) await delivery. Only 32 Albemarles I Series Is were completed as bombers with a dorsal four-gun Boulton Paul turret, as the aircraft was deemed inferior to existing types. After also being rejected for general reconnaissance duties, Albemarles were delivered for use as glider-tugs and airborne forces aircraft in General Transport (GT) or Special Transport (ST) configurations. It entered service in January 1943 with 295 Squadron, which flew its first operational missions with the aircraft in support of the invasion of Sicily in July 1943. Albemarles later participated in D-Day and supported the Arnhem operation in 1944. Production ended in December 1944 after 600 were built. Albemarles were flown by 161, 295, 296, 297, 511 and 570 Squadrons and, although little use was made of them during the war, they remained in service into February 1946. The only other operator was the Soviet Union, which received around a dozen.

HANDLEY PAGE HALTON

The Halton was a civil transport conversion of the Halifax heavy bomber. Twelve Halifax C.VIIIs were modified to accommodate ten passengers, plus 8,000lb (3,629kg) of freight in an under-fuselage pannier. Work to complete the prototype Halton I (G-AHDU) was undertaken by Short Brothers and Harland at Belfast, Northern Ireland, and the aircraft was christened *Falkirk* at Radlett, Hertfordshire, on July 18, 1946. The Halton entered service with British Overseas Airways Corporation (BOAC) to fill the gap created by the late delivery of its Avro Tudors. The fleet was used on routes to Cairo, Egypt, and Karachi, India, as well as on West African Trans-Sahara services; *Falkirk* is seen at Khartoum in Sudan in August 1946. Haltons were operated by the airline for only 12 months, the majority later going to Aviation Traders. One Halton 2 was also produced and flown by British American Air Service on behalf of the Maharajah Gaekwar of Baroda, a former Indian state in present-day Gujarat.

Britain had a lead in jet engine technology at the end of the war, but this was not matched by an exploitation of the aerodynamics that would have greatly improved performance. Plans for an aircraft to break the 'sound barrier' – the Miles M.52 – were cancelled in February 1946 and adoption of swept wing fighters was delayed until long after the US North America F-86 Sabre and Soviet Mikoyan-Gurevich MiG-15 had entered service.

By 1950, the best the RAF's Fighter Command had was the straight wing de Havilland Vampire and Gloster Meteor, both of which first flew during the war. At the same point, Bomber Command still relied on the Avro Lincoln – little more than a bigger Lancaster – and was receiving Boeing B-29 Superfortresses (as Washingtons) from America; it was only in May 1951 that it accepted its first jet bomber, the English Electric Canberra, into service.

The impetus to improve both the quantity and quality of the armed forces came when North Korean invaded its southern neighbour on 25 June 1950, beginning a brutal three-year war which saw China and the Soviet Union on one side and the United States and other members of the United Nations (including Britain) on the other. The early 1950s saw a build-up of British military forces from which the aviation industry benefited.

Aircraft for the Airlines

During World War Two, Lend-Lease also alleviated the lack of modern transport aircraft produced by British manufacturers, with the Douglas Dakota (US Army Air Force Skytrain or Skytrooper) becoming the standard RAF freight hauler by the conclusion of the conflict. As the end of the European war approached, plans were laid for the design of several classes of airliners by both the government and manufacturers, with the aim of capturing a large share of the market post-war. The immediate need for commercial airliners resulted in stopgap conversions of the Avro Lancaster and Handley Page Halifax bombers as the Lancastrian and Halton, plus modifications of Short Sunderland flying boats as Sandringhams.

In addition, existing production types (such as the Avro York) and others adopted from originally military designs (including the Bristol 170 and Vickers Viking) became the first generation of 'interim' post-war British airliners, while development of definitive types was undertaken. Unfortunately, while the demand for airliners across the globe was large, so was the number of suitable surplus military transports that could be configured for fare-paying passengers. Coupled to the slow and often troubled development of many of the post-war British airliners, this all but guaranteed that relatively few of the early designs would be built.

By the end of the 1940s, the great hope was the jet-powered de Havilland Comet, which not only offered a significant increase in performance in terms of speed, but also better passenger comfort thanks to its pressurised cabin. At the start of 1950, it appeared that the Comet would be a 'world beater', a standard bearer for the British aviation industry in the second half of the 20th century. Tragically, it was not to be.

Golden Age

The first 50 years of the 20th century was a golden age for British aviation. It encompassed the pioneering years, the great leaps forward sparked by the two world wars, the development of the airliner and the rise of private aviation. More different types of aircraft were built and flew in the British Isles during the first 50 years than in the 70 years since, while the total number of aircraft rolled out was far greater, reaching its zenith during World War Two.

Identifying the aircraft to adequately represent the period is no easy task. Although it is tempting to focus on the famous – the Sopwith Camel, de Havilland DH.60 Moth, Hawker Hurricane, Supermarine Spitfire, Avro Lancaster – for each that became a household name, numerous others never even made it into the public consciousness. They include many types that flew only as prototypes, failed to find a place in the market, or served in pedestrian roles that never generated headlines in the newspapers. The story of the first 50 years of British aviation cannot be told without them.

FLEET AIR ARM

At the end of the 1940s, the FAA was in the process of transitioning from piston- to jet-powered carrier-borne aircraft, illustrated by this mid-1949 line up of a de Havilland Sea Hornet NF.21 night fighter (foreground), de Havilland Sea Vampire F.20 and Hawker Sea Fury FB.11. In the distance, beyond the second Sea Vampire, are a Fairey Firefly FR.4 and Airspeed Oxford 'hack'. With the exception of the Oxford, a pre-war design, each of these aircraft was flown – at least as a prototype – during World War Two, although the variants depicted entered service after the conflict. Only 78 production Sea Hornet NF.21s were built between March 1948 and November 1950, serving with 809 Squadron and a number of second line units. Most of the 30 Sea Vampire F.20s were used by trials and training units; VV143 was delivered in December 1948 and eventually scrapped at Lossiemouth in Moray, Scotland, during January 1960. A total of 615 Sea Furies were built for the Royal Navy, serving as the standard fighter from its carriers into the early 1950s. Sea Fury FB.11 VW564 was delivered in September 1948 and served with the FAA until sold back to its manufacturer in December 1956.

VICKERS VIKING

Vickers created the Viking civil transport by mating a new fuselage to the wings of the Wellington bomber. The aircraft proved popular with airlines in the years immediately following World War Two and a small number were also acquired for the RAF. A contract for 45 for the RAF was placed in October 1945, but the order was subsequently modified to cover two Viking C.1s and 10 C.2s, and a prototype and 21 production Valetta C.1s (the military derivative of the airliner), while the other 11 were cancelled. The first Viking was delivered to the RAF on 4 October 1946, and all 12 Vikings had been handed over by early November 1947. Four Viking C.2s went to the King's Flight at Benson, Oxfordshire, two as four passenger VVIP aircraft (one each for the King and Queen), one as a 21-seat transport and the last as a mobile maintenance workshop. Viking C.2 VL246, seen here, was the King's aircraft, delivered in January 1947. They were first used to support the Royal tour of South Africa that began on 8 March 1947, the first of many times they transported members of the King's household overseas. Vikings were still in service when the King's Flight became the Queen's Flight, after the coronation of HM Queen Elizabeth II. One of the aircraft's last official duties was to transport the Queen during her West African tour in 1956. Viking C.2 VL246 was sold to Tradair as G-APOP in August 1958, going to Channel Airways in December 1962. It was withdrawn for use in January 1965.

CHAPTER 1

TAKING TO THE SKIES
THE PIONEERS

The foundations of the British aviation industry were laid in the years before World War One, when many of those that became its leaders built their first aeroplanes. Only six years separated the first official flight in the British Isles and the start of World War One. That initial flight, by American-born Samuel Franklin Cody in British Army Aeroplane No 1, took place at Farnborough, Hampshire, on 16 October 1908, amid a period of intense activity and interest in the brave new world of aviation. In that six-year period, approximately 180 individuals and companies in Britain designed and built aeroplanes. Most were far from successful – many failed to fly at all – and in the majority of cases they progressed no further than a single example. In November 1908, Eustace, Horace and Oswald Short formed Short Brothers Ltd in London to build aeroplanes, having previously made and sold balloons. It received an order to assemble six Wright Biplanes under licence, enabling it to claim to be the 'first manufacturers of aircraft in the world'.

AVRO ROE I

Alliott Verdon Roe was the founder (with his brother, Humphrey) and first designer of A V Roe and Co Ltd – known as Avro. He made the first sustained flight in an all-British aeroplane in July 1909 and was knighted for his services to aviation in 1929. His first design, the Roe I biplane, was built at Putney in London and taken in September 1907 to the racetrack at Brooklands, Surrey, where Roe hoped to claim a £2,500 prize offered by the owners of the course to fly around it before the end of the year. The aircraft's 9hp (6.7kW) JAP engine was not powerful enough for the biplane to take off and it only flew after being towed aloft by automobiles. It also proved to be difficult to turn. In May 1908, a 24hp (18hp) Antoinette was installed and the wing area increased by adding a stub wing between the mainplanes. Early on the morning of 8 June 1908, Roe lifted the biplane above the track under its own power, making several 'hops' of 2 to 3ft (0.61 to 0.91m), which later increased to around 150ft (45.72m). The short duration of the 'flights' resulted in Roe's claim to be the first Englishman to fly in Britain being disallowed by the Royal Aero Club; that honour went instead to John Theodore Cuthbert Moore-Brabazon in a Voisin biplane on 2 May 1909.

BRISTOL BOXKITE

Boxkite No 16 was powered by a 60hp (45kW) ENV Motor Syndicate water-cooled engine and had the extended upper wings of the military version. It was delivered to the flying school at Brooklands, Surrey. The aircraft was lent to Claude Grahame-White for an attempt on the Baron de Forest Prize, offered to the first Englishman to fly an English-built aeroplane across the English Channel. Initially worth £2,000, after Louis Blériot's successful flight from France, the money was doubled in July 1909 and offered to the pilot flying from England to the furthest point on the European continent. The Boxkite was damaged while waiting to depart from Swingate Downs near Dover, Kent, but repaired. On 18 December 1910, Grahame-White tried again, but crashed No 16 near the cliffs of Dover. A second Boxkite was loaned, but the aircraft was destroyed by fire and Grahame-White abandoned the competition, which was later claimed by Thomas Sopwith. Boxkite No 16 was rebuilt at Brooklands and, during 1911, it was used by Howard Pixton, supported by mechanic Charles Briginshaw, to claim the Manville Prize, worth £500, for an aeroplane airborne for the longest aggregate period over nine days.

AVRO TYPE D

The Type D was Avro's most successful early aeroplane, with at least six built in different configurations. The prototype first flew on 1 April 1911 and was later converted into a floatplane, becoming the first British aircraft to take off from water in April 1912. This aircraft, the fourth D, was a single-seat biplane, powered by a 45hp (34kW) Green engine with a radiator hanging vertically behind it. The aircraft was built at Avro's facility at Brownsfield Mill in Manchester and delivered to Brooklands, Surrey, on 30 September 1911, where it was first flown on 12 October. Seventeen-year-old Avro 'test pilot' Frederick Phillips Raynham used the aircraft in an attempt to claim the Michelin long distance prize, which closed on 30 October. Earlier that month, he had flown with eight hours' worth of fuel, but three days before the competition closed, the engine's carburettor iced up and Raynham came down in a sewage farm. The aircraft was repaired and then served with the Avro School, which moved to Shoreham-by-Sea, West Sussex, in October 1912 as the Avro Flying School (Brighton) Ltd. It was withdrawn from use there in May 1914.

BLACKBURN TYPE E

Civil engineer Robert Blackburn built and flew his first monoplane in April 1909. Blackburn decided to create a variant of his second monoplane, known as the Type E, to enter the 1912 Military Aeroplane Trials held at Larkhill on Salisbury Plain, Wiltshire, which aimed to find a two-seat reconnaissance aircraft for the army. The fuselage of the Type E comprised steel tubes covered with aluminium, making it the first British aircraft with an all-metal body. Two were built, with significant differences. The first was produced for Lieutenant Lawrence of The Indian Aviation Company and was a single-seater powered by a 60hp (45kW) Green engine. It was named *L'Oiseau Gris* ('the grey bird') and first flew at Filey, Yorkshire, in April 1912. The following month it was delivered to Brooklands in Surrey. While due to enter the London Aerial Derby, it was removed from the list of participants, possibly because of problems with the engine. The second Type E was a two-seater powered by a 70hp (52kW) Renault V-8 engine. Although it was hoped to enter it into the military trials, the aircraft failed to leave the ground during tests in June 1912 and was subsequently withdrawn from consideration.

AVRO TYPE F

The Avro Type F has the distinction of being the first aeroplane with an enclosed cabin. A single-seat, mid-wing monoplane, the pilot had limited view through several celluloid windows, although he could thrust his head through large circular holes when flying in conditions of poor visibility! The Type F was erected at Brooklands, Surrey, in April 1912 and the first flight, with Wilfred Parke at the controls, occurred on 1 May, powered by a 35hp (26kW) Viale five-cylinder radial engine. A circuit of Brooklands was completed two days later, and the aeroplane reached 1,000ft (305m) over Chertsey, Surrey, on 17 May. Parke had to make a forced landing at Weybridge, Surrey, on 25 May, during which the aeroplane hit a fence and turned over, albeit with little damage. It was dismantled and returned to Brooklands for repairs, but did not fly again until 13 September, when the aircraft turned over on landing and was extensively damaged. The pilot, Richard Harold Barnwell, escaped unhurt, but the accident was the end of the Avro F.

SOPWITH SCHNEIDER RACER

Of all the competitions organised during the early years of the aeroplane, the Schneider Trophy is probably the most famous. Open to all waterborne aircraft, contestants were required to fly around a fixed course with the winner recording the fastest laps. The following year the race would be held in the winning team's home country. At the second competition, held in Monaco on 20 April 1914, Great Britain was represented by a Sopwith Schneider Racer. The aeroplane was a variant of the Sopwith Tabloid, which first flew on 13 November 1913, and demonstrated such a high speed that the War Office ordered 40. Sopwith replaced the Tabloid's 80hp (60kW) Gnome Lambada with a 100hp (75kW) Gnome Monosoupape, and the wheels with a single central float to create the Schneider Racer. During taxi trials prior to its first flight, the aircraft turned over, requiring much effort to repair water damage, while a new two-float landing gear (reportedly the original float cut in half) was attached to improve stability on the water. It was shipped to Monaco on 7 April. Howard Pixton (sat on the wing) flew the aircraft to victory at the contest, recording an average speed of 86.78mph (139.66km/h). The last two laps were completed at 92mph (148km/h), a new record for a seaplane. Soon after the competition, the Admiralty ordered the Schneider, eventually receiving more than 130.

ROYAL AIRCRAFT FACTORY SE2

Although only one SE2 was produced, it was rebuilt twice, resulting in three different versions. Its main claim to fame is that it was the first British single-seat scout. Originally designated the BSI (Blériot Scout No 1), the aircraft made its first flight in early 1913 with Geoffrey de Havilland at the controls, but on 27 March 1913, it entered a spin and crashed, injuring its pilot. By then, it had been redesignated as the SE2 with an 80hp (60kW) Gnome in place of the original 100hp (75kW) unit, and a slightly modified fuselage. It was re-flown by October 1913 and handed over to the RFC (Military Wing) on 17 January 1914, going to 3 Squadron. During the summer of 1914, the SE2 was modified again, replacing the monocoque fuselage with a fabric-covered built-up unit, enlarged fin and rudder, new tailplane and elevators, smaller spinner and streamlined Rafwires for bracing. By 3 October 1914, it was back in the air, going to France 23 days later to join 3 Squadron there. The unit retained the aircraft until March 1915, but it was never reported to have engaged in air-to-air combat; it may only have been used for high-speed visual reconnaissance.

AVRO 511

Very few aeroplanes were designed specifically for military roles before World War One; the Avro 511 was one of the first built in Britain. Conceived as a single-seat fast scout with an 80hp (60kW) Gnome Monosoupape rotary engine, it was displayed at the Olympia Aero Show in London on 16–25 March 1914, where the pronounced sweepback of its wings gave rise to the unofficial names 'Arrowscout' and 'Arrowplane'. The aircraft is depicted here at Hendon in north London on 23 May, where Avro's pilot Frederick Phillips Raynham (in the cockpit) was due to compete in the Aerial Derby Race around London as number '14'. Storms postponed the race until 6 June and, while Raynham was flying back to Brooklands, Surrey, on 24 May, the engine failed. Raynham managed to glide safely to the airfield. In preparation for the rescheduled competition, the mainplanes were replaced with units without sweep and a new lightweight, skid-less landing gear fitted, prompting a change in designation to Avro 514. Unfortunately, the landing gear collapsed while taxiing at Brooklands prior to flying back to Hendon, causing damage to the airframe and engine that precluded its participation in the race. Although the Avro 514 was repaired at Manchester – and successfully flown from Southport Sands, Merseyside, in July 1914 – development ended with the outbreak of war.

CHAPTER 2

WORLD WAR ONE
WINGS OF THE GREAT WAR

At the start of the conflict, the RFC had only a handful of planes at its disposal – but this proved to be the stimulus that British aviation needed and, during the war, the industry grew beyond recognition. The RFC was formed by Royal Warrant on 13 April 1912, absorbing the Air Battalion of the Royal Engineers as the Military Wing on 13 May, commanded by Major Frederick Hugh Sykes. On 1 July 1914, the Naval Wing of the RFC came under the control of the Admiralty as the Royal Naval Air Service (RNAS), with Commander Charles Rumney Samson in charge.

Britain declared war on Germany on 4 August 1914 and, at the start of what became known as the Great War, the RFC and RNAS had fewer than 200 aeroplanes between them. Nonetheless, four RFC squadrons were deployed to France in August to support the British Expeditionary Force.

During the war, the British aviation industry expanded considerably. Orders exceeded the capacity of the manufacturers and, from 1915, many engineering and woodworking companies were organised to produce components and assemble aircraft. Together, they produced more than 55,000 airframes during the conflict, in addition to 41,000 aero engines.

The two air services of the army and navy were combined to form the RAF on 1 April 1918. By the time the Armistice came into effect on 11 November 1918, the RAF had more than 22,000 aeroplanes, with 87 operational squadrons on the Western Front and 100 in other theatres.

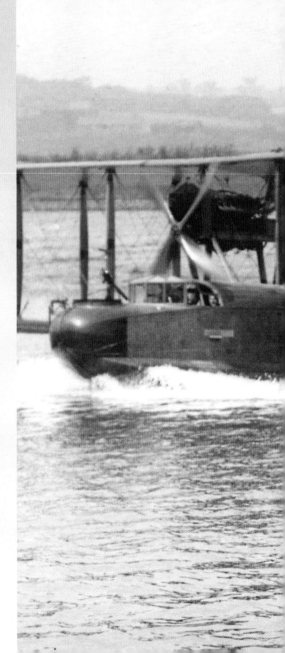

ROYAL AIRCRAFT FACTORY BE2

The BE2 was a refined version of the BE1 designed by Geoffrey de Havilland at the Royal Aircraft Factory, the sole example of which flew for the first time on 4 December 1911. More than 3,200 BE2s were built in several different subtypes, the first flying on 1 February 1912. It was judged to be the best aircraft during the Military Aeroplane Competition of August 1912, resulting in large orders being placed for assembly by various companies (as the Royal Aircraft Factory was 'only' a research organisation). Early versions were powered by Renaults, but more powerful RAF engines were used by later variants. This BE2a tested an oleo landing gear and had modified struts with a wider upper chord. A BE2 became the first RFC aircraft to land in France on 13 August 1914, a week after the start of the war. Its inherent stability made it ideal for reconnaissance over the trenches, but also easy prey for German fighters, which inflicted a terrible toll on the aircraft's crews. BE2s served with the RFC in Africa, Aden (Yemen), Palestine, Macedonia, India and on the Home Front in operational roles, as well as over the Western Front. Many remained in service when the RAF was formed in April 1918, as BE2es were flown by four frontline squadrons and nine home defence squadrons, while various training establishments still had the type. The last frontline operator was 114 Squadron at Lahore in India, which relinquished its BE2es in October 1919.

AIRCO DH.1

Geoffrey de Havilland joined The Aircraft Manufacturing Company (Airco) as chief designer in mid-1914. His first design was the DH.1, a two-seat biplane for the RFC powered by a 70hp (52kW) Renault pusher engine mounted at the rear of the fuselage nacelle, giving the gunner sitting up front a clear field of fire. De Havilland made the first flight of the prototype DH.1 (seen here) in January 1915, concluding that it had a good performance for the time. An order for 49 was placed in the spring of 1915, which was sub-let to Savages Ltd of King's Lynn, Norfolk, and the first production DH.1 arrived at Farnborough on 7 November 1915. Production aircraft differed from the prototype by having a modified, stepped cockpit, raising the pilot above the gunner, a simplified undercarriage and horizontal exhaust pipes. The majority built were fitted with a 120hp (89kW) Beardmore engine as DH.1as. A second batch of 50 was ordered from Savages, but just under half of them were completed. The DH.1/1a was obsolete by the time it entered service in significant numbers, and most were flown by training or home defence units.

WIGHT A.I IMPROVED NAVYPLANE

Designer Howard T Wright joined J Samuel White and Co of East Cowes, Isle of Wight, in 1912 and created a series of two-seat pusher floatplanes with an original wing section with 'double camber'. The most successful was the Wight 1914 Double-camber Navyplane, which was exhibited at the 1914 Olympia Aero Show in March, making its first flight on 7 April. Power was provided by a 200hp (149kW) Salmson Canton Unné radial engine. Three were ordered by the Admiralty and four for the Imperial German Navy, which only received one before the start of the war, the other three being diverted to the Royal Navy. Seven of a version with folding wings of greater span and strengthened airframe, the A.I Improved Navyplane (171 to 177), were also produced for the Admiralty. This aircraft, 176, was one of two sent to the Dardanelles to operate from seaplane carrier HMS *Ark Royal*, joining the ship at Mudros on the island of Lemnos in the North Aegean on 5 April 1915. It was used to conduct reconnaissance flights over the Turkish lines before being condemned as no longer serviceable on 14 July.

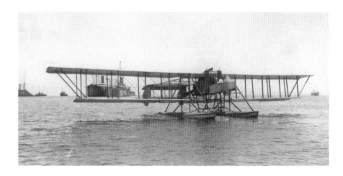

SHORT 184

The Admiralty was quick to appreciate that torpedo-carrying aircraft could be militarily useful. Short designed the Admiralty 184 Type Tractor Biplane Seaplane to carry a 14in (35.6cm) torpedo, two prototypes of which were ordered in July 1914. Like many early aircraft for the Royal Navy, it was designated after the military markings allocated to the first (184), but was also known as the Short 225, after the horsepower of the Sunbeam Mohawk installed in the prototypes. Short 184 No 184 was delivered to Isle of Grain, Kent, on 21 April 1915, and was accepted by the Admiralty the next day, before going to Felixstowe, Suffolk, at the end of the month for evaluation and trials on the seaplane tender HMS *Riviera*. On 21 May, No 184 embarked on HMS *Ben-my-Chree*, one of the two Short 184s on the steam-powered seaplane carrier when it headed for the Dardanelles, arriving at Lesbos on 10 June. The aircraft were primarily used to observe naval gunfire supporting troops ashore, as well as flying general reconnaissance sorties. On 12 August, Flight Commander Charles Humphrey Kingsman Edmonds attacked a Turkish ship in the Sea of Marmora in 184, the first ever attack with an aerial torpedo. The target had already beached, however, as it had earlier been torpedoed by the submarine E14. Edmonds successfully attacked a 5,000-ton ship on 17 August in the second Short 184 of HMS *Ben-my-Chree*. He was accompanied by Flight Lieutenant George Bentley Dacre flying 184, but problems with the aircraft's engine forced him to alight on the water in the Dardanelles. While taxiing back to the seaplane carrier, Dacre found and torpedoed a large steam tugboat in False Bay. With the weight of the torpedo gone, Dacre managed to coax the Short 184 back into the air, although the Sunbeam stopped when he was within gliding distance of his home ship. On 5 September, HMS *Ben-my-Chree* transferred its aircraft to the SS *Tringa* for transport home, 184 later going into store at the Central Supply Depot at White City, London.

SOPWITH 1½ STRUTTER

The Sopwith 1½ Strutter was the first British two-seat tractor fighter and also the first with a machine gun synchronised to fire through the arc of the propeller. Developed from the 'Sigrist Bus' as the LCT (Land Clerget Tractor), which flew in December 1915, the aircraft entered production for the Admiralty as the Type 9400 (two-seat fighter/reconnaissance) and Type 9700 (single-seat bomber), as well as for the RFC. Its unofficial 1½ Strutter name came from the pair of short and long struts (forming a 'W') between the fuselage and upper wing. Around 1,440 were built in Britain and between 4,000 and 4,500 in France for the Aéronautique Militaire as a two-seat reconnaissance aircraft (SOP 1A.2) and two- or single-seat bomber (SOP 1B.2 and 1B.1). Three SOP 1A.2s (probably including *Yen A Bon*) were assigned to the Nieuport-equipped Escadrille N23 in mid-1916, when it was based at Vadelaincourt near Verdun. The unit's commander, Captain Louis Robert de Beauchamp, had them modified as single-seaters to carry bombs and increase range. De Beauchamp and Lieutenant Pierre Daucourt used them to attack the Krupp works at Essen, Germany, on 24 September 1916, each dropping six bombs on the armament factory and returning to base unharmed, having flown more than 435 miles (700km).

BRISTOL S2A

The S2A was a development of the Scout D produced in response to an Admiralty requirement for a two-seat fighter but rejected in favour of the Sopwith 1½ Strutter. Two prototypes were ordered (as 7836 and 7837) for evaluation as advanced trainers by the War Office. They had a cockpit in which the pilot and gunner sat side by side, giving rise to its nicknames 'the sociable' and 'tubby', and were powered by 110hp (82kW) Clerget engines. The S2As first flew in May and June 1916, going to the Central Flying School at Upavon, Wiltshire. The second aircraft later went to Gosport, Hampshire, fitted with a 100hp (75hp) Gnome Monosoupape with a modified cowling. In 1923, Captain Frank Barnwell, then chief designer at Bristol, instituted retrospective design numbers for British & Colonial Aeroplane (Bristol) aircraft; the S2A became the Type 8.

BEARDMORE WB.III

The Sopwith Pup was one of the most successful fighters of World War One, serving with both the RFC and RNAS and foreign air arms. Several different variants were produced, including the Beardmore WB.III (seen here) designed to operate from warships, with manually folded wings. This aircraft (9950) was the last of a batch of 50 Pups (Admiralty Type 9901) ordered from Sir William Beardmore & Co and built at Dalmuir, Glasgow. It was officially accepted on 7 February 1917, after delivery by rail to the RNAS facility at Eastchurch in Kent. It suffered a forced landing at Allhallows on the Hoo Peninsula, Kent, on 10 March, but was recovered and repaired, only to be dismantled in May 1917. Two contracts were placed for a total of 100 production WB.IIIs. At least two retained the folding landing gear of the prototype as SB3Fs, the rest being SB3Ds with a jettisonable undercarriage and flotation gear.

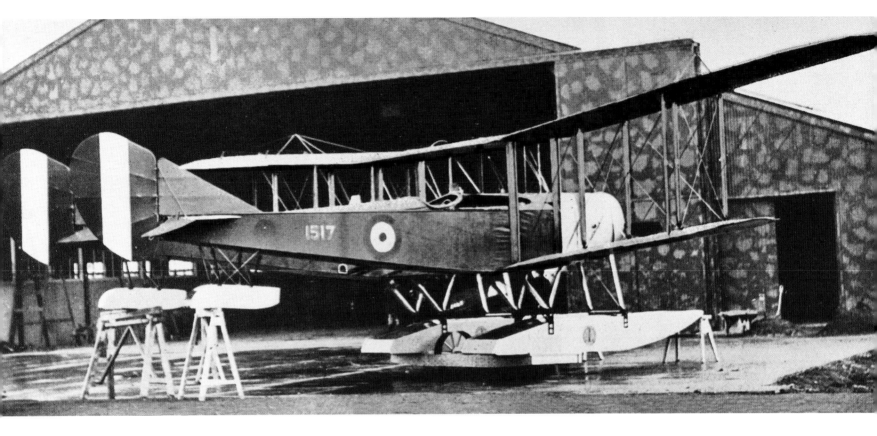

BLACKBURN TB

In March 1915, the Admiralty placed an order for nine Blackburn TB anti-Zeppelin fighters. The requirement called for a two-seat aircraft with long range that could fly at night, climb above a German airship and drop incendiary darts to ignite the hydrogen in its gas cells. The Blackburn TB (Twin Blackburn) was designed to have two Smith Static radial engines, but problems with that engine resulted in the substitution of Gnome Monosoupape 9Bs, delivering only two-thirds of the horsepower originally expected. The aircraft's unusual configuration, with two fuselages and cockpits, made communication between the pilot and observer difficult, as they had to resort to hand signals. The first TB flew in August 1915 and was joined by two more (including one powered by Clergets) for evaluation by the RNAS at Isle of Grain in Kent during 1916. The reduction in expected power greatly impacted the rate of climb, ceiling and weight of darts that could be carried, making the TB unsuitable for its stated mission. In June 1916, Blackburn was told to store the airframes until the Smith engine was available. The engines failed to materialise and, during 1917, the TBs were broken up.

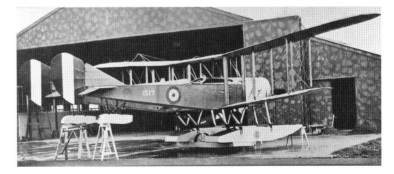

SOPWITH TRIPLANE

The Triplane was developed from the Sopwith Pup, the most significant difference being the use of three sets of narrow chord wings, all with ailerons, giving it great manoeuvrability. The first of two Triplane prototypes was flown by Harry Hawker at Brooklands, Surrey, early in June 1916. Orders were placed by the Admiralty for 180 and by the War Office for 266, but the contracts for the RFC were cancelled and only 145 production aircraft were built for the RNAS, comprising 95 from Sopwith, 47 by Clayton & Shuttleworth and three by Oakley of Ilford, Essex. Triplane N5420 was the first production aircraft built by Sopwith at Kingston upon Thames, Surrey, initially going to Clayton & Shuttleworth in Lincoln, Lincolnshire, for use as a pattern for their own assembly line. On 9 November 1916, it arrived at Koksijde near Furnes in Belgium for Naval A Squadron for operational trials. James Earle Minifie flew the aircraft on 12 December to St Omer, France, to be demonstrated to the RFC. There it was involved in a ground accident that damaged the airframe and required a new engine. During a post-repair test flight on 18 December, the Triplane crashed, badly injuring Minifie. The airframe went to Dunkirk without its Clerget engine and was deleted from the inventory on 24 February 1917. Triplanes were flown by five naval squadrons on the Western Front, most famously by 'Black Flight' of 10 Naval Squadron but had largely been withdrawn by mid-1917.

DeH.5. 110. Le Rhone.

AIRCO DH.5

The Airco DH.5 was a single-seat tractor biplane scout-fighter designed in late 1916 for the RFC. Its most unusual feature was the backwards stagger of the upper wing, designed so the pilot had a clear view forward and upwards, although limiting it to the rear. The unmarked prototype (which later became A5172, as depicted) first flew at Hendon in north London in August 1916, later gaining a reprofiled fin and rudder and a single Vickers machine gun offset to port that could be elevated 60° to attack aircraft from below. An order for 200 was placed with Airco (one later cancelled), plus 200 from the Darracq Motor Engineering Company, 50 from the British Caudron Company and 100 (38 built) from March, Jones & Cribb. The swivelling machine gun was replaced with a fixed forward-firing unit with Constantinesco gun interrupter gear so it could fire through the propeller's arc, which proved troublesome in service. The first unit to receive DH.5s was 24 Squadron on 1 May 1917, with 32 Squadron taking deliveries later the same month. Other squadrons that flew DH.5s were 41, 64, 68 and 65, the latter the final one to convert to the type in October 1917. Poor performance at altitude resulted in the DH.5 being relegated to 'trench strafing', notably during the first Battle of Ypres. Surviving aircraft were withdrawn from frontline duties by March 1918, many returning from France being re-issued to training units in the UK.

DeH.5. 110. Le Rhone.

ROYAL AIRCRAFT FACTORY RE8

Known as the 'Harry Tate' by its crews, the RE8 had a good turn of speed and a useful operational ceiling but was inherently stable, reducing its manoeuvrability and making it a sitting target for German fighters. More than 4,050 were built for the RFC and it served as the standard two-seat reconnaissance and artillery-spotting aircraft until the Armistice, at times suffering appalling losses. The first unit to re-equip with the RE8, 52 Squadron, arrived in France on 21 November 1916. Several early aircraft were lost in accidents, resulting in a temporary withdrawal while rectification work was undertaken, with later aircraft having a redesigned larger tail to reduce its tendency to spin, although the RE8 was subsequently viewed with suspicion by its crews. The lack of suitable replacements kept the RE8 in service longer than it should have been, and, on the day the RAF was formed, it was flown by 21 squadrons in France, Italy, Mesopotamia, Palestine and Ireland. It is believed RE8s accumulated the highest number of flying hours over France of any RFC aircraft. RE8 A3916 was one of 400 built by D Napier & Son at Acton in west London. It was taken on charge by the RFC in September 1917.

SOPWITH CAMEL

Although difficult to master and often fatal in the hands of inexperienced pilots, the Sopwith Camel was highly manoeuvrable and is credited with destroying more enemy aircraft during World War One – nearly 1,300 – than any other Allied fighter. Originally conceived as a 'Big Pup', the Sopwith F.1 got its unofficial name from the 'hump' covering the gun breeches. Harry Hawker flew the prototype for the first time on 22 December 1916 from Brooklands, Surrey. An order for 250 F.1s was placed by the War Office in May 1917 and a total of just under 5,700 were eventually built in three major versions. Most were completed as F.1 fighters. A naval variant was developed in 1918 as the 2F.1 Ship's Camel, designed to operate from the larger warships of the Royal Navy and towed lighters. It had a fuselage built in two halves, so it could be disassembled for storage afloat, and slightly shorter wings. Only one of the F.1's two Vickers machine guns was retained, while a trainable Lewis gun was mounted on the upper wing. The first flew as early as March 1917 and around 230 were built by five companies, including N6635 by Sopwith, seen at Brooklands. Ship's Camels were used by the Home Fleet to attack airships and floatplanes over the North Sea. The third Camel production variant was the TF.1, an armoured 'trench fighter'.

FELIXSTOWE F3

The Felixstowe flying boats earned an enviable reputation during the final year of World War One and the immediate post-war years. The first Felixstowe F2As were delivered to the RNAS in late 1917 to patrol the coastal waters from Felixstowe, Suffolk, and Great Yarmouth, Norfolk, searching for enemy shipping, including U-boats and Zeppelins. F2As frequently met and fought with enemy aircraft, with one three-hour battle involving four F2As and a Curtiss H12 against 14 hostile seaplanes, during which the British flying boats shot down six enemy aircraft for the loss of one F2A. The F3 first flew in February 1917 and could carry more bombs further than the F2A but was slower and less manoeuvrable. Unlike the F2A, it operated in the Mediterranean as well as over home waters. This F3 (N4002) operated from Tresco in the Scilly Islands from late August 1918 with 350 Flight (later part of 234 Squadron), guarding the Western Approaches to the English Channel. The final version was the F5. It entered RAF service after the Armistice with 230 and 231 Squadrons, the latter unit disbanding on 7 July 1919. On 1 April 1923, 230 Squadron became 480 Flight based at Calshot, Hampshire, continuing to fly F5s until 1925.

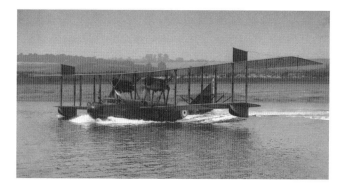

BOULTON & PAUL P.3 BOBOLINK

Boulton & Paul Ltd of Norwich, Norfolk – named after partners William Staples Boulton and Joseph Paul – began aeronautical construction in 1915, assembling other company's aircraft, notably Sopwith Camels. A design department was later established, and its first aircraft was the P.3 Bobolink, designed to Specification A.1A as a replacement for the Camel. Originally known as the Boblink, the P.3 was rechristened the Bobolink (after a North American bird species). One of its unusual features was that the pilot could jettison either (or both) of the two fuel tanks, which were located behind the cockpit and separated by armour, in case of fire. Three Bobolinks were ordered, to be powered by the Bentley BR2, the prototype (C8655) rolling out in December 1917 prior to installation of its engine. After being fitted with the fourth BR2 built, the Bobolink was flown by company test pilot Captain Frank Courtney at Mousehold in Norwich, in early 1918, after which ailerons (originally only on the upper mainplane, as seen here) were added to the lower wings to improve manoeuvrability. It was also noted that the Bobolink had poor ground handling. During March 1918, the prototype was evaluated against the Austin Osprey, Nieuport BN.1 and Sopwith Snipe, resulting in the latter being selected for production. Following the official trials, the two outstanding Bobolinks were cancelled and work on the design ceased.

AIRCO (DE HAVILLAND) DH.9A

The DH.9A was a stalwart of the RAF in its formative years. It was developed from the disappointing DH.9 by increasing the span and chord of the mainplanes and ailerons and installing a more powerful engine. By mid-February 1918, Airco had modified DH.9 C6350 as the first DH.9A, powered by a Rolls-Royce Eagle VIII. It was evaluated at Martlesham Heath, Suffolk, from 23 February. As a shortage of Eagle VIIIs resulted in the adoption of the American Liberty 12, Airco passed responsibility for integration of the engine and production of DH.9A airframes to Westland Aircraft, although assembly was widely sub-contracted. The first Liberty-powered DH.9A flew on 19 April 1918. In June 1918, 110 Squadron became the first to re-equip with (Eagle-powered) DH.9As, the unit deploying to the Western Front on 31 August in the day-bomber role. It was later joined in France by 18, 99 and 205 Squadrons. Westland-built F1067 is understood to have been taken on charge by the RAF in September 1918 and served with 18 Squadron around the time of the Armistice. Its service career may have been short, as it was no longer in the RAF's inventory by 1920. The RAF had accepted 885 DH.9As by the end of 1918, but total production reached more than 2,140 (including rebuilt examples), with Parnall receiving the final contract for new aircraft in January 1927. DH.9As remained in RAF service into 1931.

MARTINSYDE F.4 BUZZARD

Many outstanding aircraft were developed during 1918, several of which had their service careers curtailed by the Armistice. The Martinsyde F.4 Buzzard fell into this category and, although 338 were built, it is largely overlooked today. The F.4 was a development of the F.3 powered by a 300hp (224kW) Hispano Suiza 8, as the Rolls-Royce Falcon III of the earlier aircraft was not available, with its cockpit repositioned 10in (25.4cm) further aft, improving the pilot's view. The prototype was tested at Martlesham Heath, Suffolk, in June 1918, during which performance was demonstrated to be superior to the rival Sopwith Snipe – the Buzzard was 10 per cent faster, had a 38 per cent quicker climb and a 35 per cent higher ceiling. Martinsyde was rewarded with an order for 150, later increased to 450, plus three long-range Mk IAs, while contracts for a further 1,000 were placed with Boulton & Paul, Hooper, and Standard Motors. Only 57 had reached the RAF by the Armistice, none of which were issued to operational squadrons. Post-war, the Snipe was adopted by the RAF instead, having the benefit of being 25 per cent cheaper than the Buzzard, available in greater numbers and already with the squadrons. Martinsyde was allowed to complete the Buzzards it had started building. The company ceased operations in 1923, with many Buzzards passing to the Aircraft Disposal Co. The manufacturer and liquidator supplied Buzzard variants to Belgium, Bolivia, Canada, Finland (15), Ireland (four), Japan (one), Latvia (eight), Lithuania (two), Poland (one), Portugal (four), Spain (30) and the Soviet Union (around 100), while others went to private operators.

CHAPTER 3

THE 1920S

SWORDS TO PLOUGHSHARES

With war behind them, aircraft manufacturers facing a lean period needed to find alternative markets if they were to have any kind of a future. It was hoped that demand from private operators would keep the production lines open.

In the years immediately following World War One, around 2,000 surplus British military aeroplanes were sold via the Aircraft Disposal Company, which was established in March 1920. Although many were purchased by governments overseas, this glut of cheap aeroplanes made it extremely difficult for the numerous manufacturers that had prospered during the conflict to market new designs to the private owner or operator. Most companies struggled to remain in business in the first half of the 1920s, with several branching out to produce automobiles or machinery in order to survive. Those that remained in business were rewarded from the second half of the decade with growing sales to the expanding number of aero clubs.

VICKERS VIMY

Designed to bomb Berlin, the Vickers FB27 Vimy became famous for its use on long-distance pioneering flights. The first Vimy made its maiden flight on 30 November 1917 at Joyce Green near Dartford, London, but the war ended before it could enter service, cutting production to just over 200 aircraft. Hoping to secure the £10,000 offered by the *Daily Mail* newspaper for the first direct crossing of the Atlantic, Vickers modified the thirteenth Vimy produced at Brooklands, Surrey, with extra fuel tanks. After test flying it on 18 April 1919, the aircraft was crated and shipped to St John's, Newfoundland, Canada, to take advantage of the prevailing westerly winds. Captain John Alcock and Lieutenant Arthur Whitten Brown departed Lester's Field (as seen here) in the aircraft on 14 June, coming down in a bog at Clifden, County Galway, Ireland, after flying for 15hrs and 57mins. Both were knighted soon after the flight and, on 15 December, the Vimy was handed over to the Science Museum in South Kensington, London, where it remains on display. Between 12 November and 10 December 1919, Ross and Keith Smith, with mechanics James Bennett and Wally Shiers, became the first to fly between Britain and Australia in a Vimy IV.

ROYAL AIRCRAFT FACTORY SE5

Four SE5as lined up at the start of the Varsity Air Race between Oxford and Cambridge universities held on 16 July as part of the 1921 Aerial Derby at Hendon in north London. Eight SE5as were hired from the Aircraft Disposal Co and acquired the universities' colours for the event – four in dark blue for Oxford and four in light blue for Cambridge. SE5a F5258 was registered as G-EAXT on 4 July 1921, receiving the race number '26'; it was cancelled from the register on 13 November 1922. Number '25' was G-EAXV, the former F5253, which was cancelled on 17 July 1922. Three aircraft from each team competed, flying three laps of a 40-mile (64km) circuit. One of the Oxford team (Mr N Pring) had to retire during the race, force-landing into a field near Enfield in north London. Cambridge's pilots adopted the tactic of gaining height, seeking cooler air to improve the performance of the SE5a's Wolseley Viper engine. It worked, as the team came home in first, second and third places. Unfortunately, the race was never repeated.

H 12

SHORT SILVER STREAK

The Short Swallow – later renamed Silver Streak – was the first all-metal aeroplane built in Britain. It was produced because one of the Short brothers, Hugh Oswald, believed that the aluminium alloy duralumin was a better material for constructing aeroplanes, being stronger and more resistant to fire and rot than wood and fabric. Unable to convince the Air Ministry to fund the project, Short Brothers used their own funds in 1919 to design and build the Swallow. Duralumin was used throughout for the frames of the semi-monocoque fuselage and wings and for the stress skins riveted to them. Power was provided by a 240hp (179kW) Puma. The Swallow was a single-seater, with a cargo compartment for up to 400lb (181kg) forward of the cockpit. It was registered as G-EARQ on 17 March 1920, but the markings were not painted on the aircraft. Short Brothers displayed the Swallow soon after completion at Olympia in London from 9 July, after which the name was changed to Silver Streak. Test pilot John Lankester Parker made the first flight at Grain in Kent on 20 August, after which the Silver Streak was grounded so that the skins of the wings and tailplane could be replaced. It was sold to the Air Ministry on 23 December 1920, becoming J6854, flying again after work was completed on 27 January 1921. Five days later, it arrived at Farnborough, Hampshire, for evaluation by the RAE. On 6 June, its landing gear was damaged during a forced landing, after which the airframe was relegated to static and vibration tests. It was scrapped in December 1923.

DE HAVILLAND DH.50

The DH.50 was a four-passenger cabin biplane, the prototype first flying on 30 July 1923. A total of 38 were built, of which de Havilland produced 17, while Aero, in then-Czechoslovakia, assembled seven and SABCA, in Belgium, three. Three organisations in Australia – Qantas, Western Australian Airways and Larkin Aircraft – were responsible for the other 11, the type proving popular in that country. One British-built DH.50A was ordered for the Governor General of Australia, Lord Stonehaven, but was used by the Royal Australian Air Force (RAAF) instead (as A8-1, seen here) as a survey aircraft with interchangeable float/ wheel landing gears. It was handed over at Rochester, Kent, on 26 March 1926 and tested at Point Cook in Victoria on 11 September, fitted with floats in preparation for a survey of the southwest Pacific, including New Guinea and the Solomon Islands. Flown by Flight Lieutenant Ivor Ewing McIntyre and Group Captain Richard Williams (the Chief-of-the-Air Staff of the RAAF) with mechanic Flight Sergeant Les Trist, it was the first overseas mission by an aircraft and crew of the air force. Between late September and 7 December, the trio flew more than 10,000 miles (16,093km), returning safely to Point Cook, where they were welcomed back by 12 aircraft of the RAAF and a 300-man honour guard. The DH.50A, refitted with a wheel landing gear, was also flown by Williams around Australia between 21 July and 10 September 1927, accompanied by a pair of de Havilland DH.9As, the three aircraft covering almost 13,000 miles (20,921km).

DE HAVILLAND DH.66 HERCULES

Before Imperial Airways took over the Cairo, Egypt, to Baghdad, Iraq, route from the RAF, it needed a new long-distance airliner. The de Havilland DH.66 was designed for the service, able to carry seven passengers and the mail; the name Hercules was selected after a competition held in the *Meccano Magazine*. Three Bristol Jupiter VI radial engines were installed to reduce the risk of a forced landing in the desert, while fabric-covered tubular steel construction was used for the fuselage so that it would not deteriorate in the heat. Imperial Airways ordered five and the prototype (G-EBMW) was first flown by Hubert Stanford Broad on 30 September 1926 at de Havilland's premises at Stag Lane in Edgware, London. In 1929, the airline ordered a further pair and an additional four were delivered to Western Australian Airways with cabins for 14 passengers, the six Hercules differing from the original aircraft by having an enclosed cockpit and a tailwheel in place of the original skid. Both features were later retrofitted to the first five Hercules, as seen here on the prototype, depicted flying with one engine shut down. When Imperial Airways withdrew the airliner in 1935, three were acquired by the South African Air Force, which continued to fly two into 1943.

AVRO AVENGER

The Avro 566 Avenger (seen here) was designed by Roy Chadwick as a private venture single-seat fighter. It made use of an oval section semi-monocoque fuselage, a feature unique in its day. Herbert 'Bert' Hinkler piloted the Avenger on its maiden flight at Hamble, Hampshire, on 26 June 1926, and the following week it appeared at the RAF Display at Hendon, north London. Between October and December 1926, the Avenger was evaluated at Avro's request at Martlesham Heath, Suffolk, the RAF test establishment. While low-level performance was praised, the Napier Lion VIII engine proved troublesome, and the RAF had little interest in the Avenger. Chadwick had designed it to accept wings with different characteristics for a number of different roles to increase its appeal to overseas customers. In May 1928, it was fitted with narrower, equal span wings, each with ailerons, while the landing gear was revised. At the same time, the engine was replaced by a more powerful Lion IX and the wooden two blade propeller gave way to a metal unit with a smaller spinner. In this form, the aircraft became the Avro 567 Avenger II. It was faster and more manoeuvrable, but although demonstrated to the Romanian authorities in September 1928, no production contract was forthcoming. From May 1931, the Avenger II became an instructional airframe with Air Service Training at Hamble.

BLACKBURN LINCOCK

The F2 Lincock I was one of the most manoeuvrable fighters of its time – despite the low power of its Armstrong Siddeley Lynx IV engine – and was blessed with good handling. It was unveiled to the press at Blackburn's airfield at Brough in the East Riding of Yorkshire on 15 May 1928. By the time of the 1928 King's Cup Race in July, during which the Lincock I came tenth at an average speed of 115.32mph (185.6km/h), the cylinder heads were covered, but as this caused the Lynx to overheat, they were soon removed. In the summer of 1930, the aircraft was painted light blue for a tour of the United States, flown by Lieutenant Richard Llewellyn Roger Atcherley, during which it participated in the American National Air Races at Cleveland, Ohio. After returning to Britain, the aircraft continued to fly until the end of July 1931; it was subsequently dismantled at Brough. The Mk I was followed by a F2A Lincock II in 1929, with a metal airframe instead of its predecessor's wooden construction, a new tail profile and the gap between the fuselage and lower wing faired over. Five generally similar F2D Lincock IIIs were then produced, with China and Japan both taking two, while the fifth went to Sir Alan Cobham's aerial circus. In addition, the Italian company Piaggio built one under licence as the P.II in 1932.

BRISTOL 110A

Bristol exhibited its Type 110A (G-AAFG) at the 1929 Olympia Aero Show held in London in July prior to its first flight. Designed to appeal to charter operators, the aircraft could carry up to four passengers in a cabin in addition to the pilot. It could be powered by a number of different engine models, making its debut at Olympia with a mock-up of the seven-cylinder 315hp (235kW) Bristol Neptune, which had been replaced by a five-cylinder 220hp (164kW) Bristol Titan for its first flight on 25 October 1929. A Neptune was installed in January 1930, but the aircraft was damaged while landing early in the following month. With no orders forthcoming, Bristol decided to cease work on the aircraft and the prototype was scrapped.

DE HAVILLAND DH.60 MOTH

The most successful light aircraft produced between the wars by the British aviation industry was the de Havilland DH.60 Moth family. A two-seat biplane, initially of wooden construction, the prototype Moth first flew at Stag Lane in north London on 22 February 1925, in the hands of Geoffrey de Havilland. It was powered by an ADC Cirrus engine, as were early production aircraft, known as Cirrus Moths. A change to the Cirrus Hermes and a larger wingspan created the Cirrus II Moth, while a handful had the Armstrong Siddeley Genet as Genet Moths. The majority of Moths were powered by the de Havilland Gipsy I or II engines as DH.60Gs, just under 600 of which were built at Stag Lane. Most Gipsy Moths were DH.60M 'Metal Moths', which had fuselages with metal (rather than wooden) stringers. A further 134 Moths were completed as DH.60GIII variants, powered by the Gipsy III. Gipsy Moth G-AARI was initially retained by de Havilland as a demonstrator from late 1929, being sold privately in July 1930 and based at Heston, Hounslow, in London. It was sold overseas in early 1933.

BLACKBURN BLUEBIRD

Although little known today, the Blackburn L1C Bluebird IV was a popular light aircraft in its time. The all-metal light biplane was Blackburn's response to the de Havilland DH.60 Moth series for the private or club flyer, marketing placing much emphasis on its side-by-side seating (as opposed to its competitor's tandem cockpits). Unfortunately, the Bluebird IV failed to match the sales success of the Moth, as only 58 were produced. The first of three built at Brough, East Yorkshire, flew in March 1929, but, as Blackburn was busy with military production, it reached an agreement with Saunders-Roe in June 1929 to assemble the Bluebird at its Solent Works on the west bank of the Medina on the Isle of Wight, with test flights undertaken from Somerton, Hampshire. Saunders-Roe built 55 Bluebird IVs, although a handful of that total were finished at Brough after May 1931. Bluebird IVs were frequent participants in the various air races around Britain (as seen here) in the 1930s and were also the mounts for some notable long-distance flights. Mrs Victor Bruce (Mildred Mary Bruce) flew G-ABDS around the world eastwards between September 1930 and February 1931, the Bluebird being transported by ship across the Atlantic and Pacific oceans. Lieutenant Commander G A Hall, of the Royal Australian Navy, piloted G-AAVG from Croydon, London, to Wyndham, Western Australia, in 24 days from 8 August 1932.

GLOSTER AS.31 SURVEY

Aerial survey was regarded as a key to developing the British dominions and colonies in the early 1920s. The official contractors to the Ordnance Survey, the Aircraft Operating Company, used converted de Havilland DH.9s in the role, but, by 1926, a replacement was required, and a specification was written by the organisation. A twin-engined aircraft of metal construction that could, in an emergency, be broken down for transport was outlined. It had to be able to maintain 9,000ft (2,743m) on one engine with a full load. De Havilland responded with the DH.67B, but construction of the aircraft passed to Gloster, which refined it to produce the AS.31 Survey, powered by two 525hp (391kW) Bristol Jupiter XIs. Two prototypes were built. The first (G-AADO) flew in June 1929 and, in March 1930, departed for South Africa for a survey of the Zambezi Basin. It was used over Northern Rhodesia (now Zambia) and Central Africa before being sold to the South African Air Force as 250. The AS.31 was operated by the air force's photographic section until withdrawn from service in 1942. The second aircraft (K2602) was used by the Air Ministry at Farnborough, Hampshire, between November 1931 and September 1936.

CHAPTER 4

THE 1920S

THE RISE OF THE SILVER
BIPLANE

Multiple adaptations, a plethora of prototypes and a determination to break records were very much in the spirit of the Roaring Twenties. It was also a time to wave farewell to types that had had their day in the sun.

At the end of World War One, the RAF had more than 22,000 aeroplanes and the Air Ministry had issued orders for many thousands more. Most outstanding contracts were cancelled soon after the Armistice, although some companies were permitted to complete aircraft on which construction had reached a sufficiently advanced stage. The vast network of firms from outside the industry, many subcontracted to assemble complete aircraft that had been designed by another manufacturer, was no longer needed, with most returning to their pre-war activities. In August 1919, the British government adopted the guideline that the Empire would not be engaged in another 'great' war for at least ten years and funding for the armed forces was cut. More than 10,000 aeroplanes were sold to the Aircraft Disposal Company in 1920. By 1924, the RAF had around 480 front- and 500 second-line aeroplanes, and although these figures had doubled by 1929, major production contracts were few and competition for them was fierce. Any specification released by the Air Ministry for a new aircraft generated responses from several manufacturers, creating many one-off prototypes that failed to enter production. Throughout the 1920s, RAF aircraft became more colourful. The drab camouflage of World War One slowly disappeared and silver finishes became ubiquitous, while fighter squadrons applied striking markings to their aircraft. The 1920s and early 1930s were the heyday of the RAF's silver biplane.

SOPWITH 7F.1 SNIPE

The Snipe was a development of the Sopwith Camel, the first prototype of which was built as a private venture, powered by the 150hp (112kW) Bentley BR1, with its best feature the high cockpit giving the pilot a better view. When the more powerful Bentley BR2 became available, it was installed on the second prototype Snipe and a contract for six prototypes was secured from the War Office. These were evaluated at Martlesham Heath, Suffolk, resulting in initial contracts for more than 1,700 Snipes being issued to seven contractors, which were soon followed by additional orders. Snipes entered service with 43 Squadron on the Western Front in August 1918, followed by 201 and 4 Squadrons of the Australian Flying Corps, while 208 was in the process of converting to the fighter at the time of the Armistice. Major William George Barker won the Victoria Cross on 27 October 1918, after taking on 15 Fokker DVIIs single-handedly in Snipe E8102, shooting down three, despite being wounded. Around 2,170 Snipes were completed, and it became the standard day fighter in the post-war RAF, with 25 Squadron the sole fighter unit on home defence duties between April 1920 and November 1922. Snipe E8057 was one of a batch of 300 built by Sopwith, all delivered by March 1919. It was with 70 Squadron based at Grantham, Lincolnshire, from February 1919, but suffered a ground-loop later that year. Snipes were replaced in operational squadrons in Britain in May 1926 but were used by 1 Squadron in Iraq until November that year and by second-line units a little while longer.

AVRO 504L

More than 11,000 Avro 504s were built between 1913 and 1932. It served as a fighter and bomber during World War One – and was the most produced British aircraft of the conflict – as well as a trainer, a role that it continued to be used for into the late 1930s with the RAF. Many different variants were made in Britain, as well as in Japan, the Soviet Union and other countries. The Avro 504L was a floatplane version of the 504K designed for seaplane training. This is the prototype C4329, on the beach at Hamble, Hampshire, in early 1919, with the four-strut undercarriage initially used and 130hp (97kW) Clerget engine. Although the prototype was a two-seater, most of the approximately 30 that followed (many conversions of existing airframes) could carry three people and were powered by the 150hp (112kW) Bentley BR1 rotary engine. Avro 504Ls were delivered to Australia, Canada, Chile, Japan, New Zealand and the USSR. Avro Transport Co and The Eastbourne Aviation Co also flew them on joy flights along the English south coast in the early 1920s.

HANDLEY PAGE O/400

The origins of the O/400 stemmed from a request passed to Frederick Handley Page by Captain Murray Sueter, director of the Air Department of the Royal Navy, from the naval officer Charles Rumney Samson for 'a bloody paralyser of an airplane' for long-range bombing. The outcome was the O/100, the first of four prototypes flying on 17 December 1915, followed by 42 production aircraft for the RNAS. Further development resulted in the O/400, which substituted the more powerful Rolls-Royce Eagle VIII engine in place of the Eagle II/IV, a strengthened fuselage, increased bomb load and revised fuel system. Deliveries to the RNAS were planned to start in March 1918, but were delayed until the following month, after the RAF had been created. Three former RNAS units – 207, 214 and 215 Squadrons – were the first to receive O/400s, replacing their O/100s between April and June 1918, forming part of the Independent Air Force tasked with striking industrial targets in the Rhine and Saar regions of Germany. Before the end of the war, they were joined by 58, 97, 100, 115 and 216 Squadrons, but with the signing of the Armistice, the O/400 force was quickly run down. This aircraft, B8811, served with 207 Squadron in Germany as part of the Army of Occupation during 1919. Around 550 O/400s were built in Britain, while the Standard Aircraft Corporation assembled 107 under licence in the US.

ARMSTRONG WHITWORTH SINAIA

Siddeley-Deasy of Coventry, Warwickshire, received a contract for four Sinaia I day bombers in February 1918. Power was to be provided by a pair of Siddeley Tigers, a V-12 water-cooled engine that suffered considerable delays during its development, resulting in the order being cut to two aircraft. The most interesting feature of the Sinaia was the extension of the engine nacelles to incorporate a position for a defensive gunner. By the time the first – and as it turned out, only – Sinaia, J6858, made its maiden flight at Farnborough, Hampshire, on 25 June 1921, Siddeley-Deasy had become part of the Sir W G Armstrong Whitworth Aircraft Company. The Sinaia was the Tiger's first application and it proved troublesome, problems with the engine frequently interrupting the bomber's flight trials. The second aircraft, J6859, was delivered to Farnborough but never flew, instead becoming a spares source for the first. During October 1921, the Sinaia was overstressed and its fuselage buckled, ending its flight career; it was scrapped in March 1922.

ARMSTRONG WHITWORTH AWANA

Two Armstrong Whitworth Awana troop carriers were built to Specification 5/20 (originally Directorate of Research Type 12), configured to carry up to 25 troops, plus a pilot and navigator, over 400 miles (644km). The specification also required the aircraft to be able to operate from rough airstrips and stipulated folding wings for storage. Power was provided by a pair of Napier Lion II inline piston engines, while the fuselage was of tubular steel construction mated to wooden wings. The prototype, J6897, which was originally painted incorrectly as 'J6860', first flew on 28 June 1923. During its four-month evaluation by the RAF at the Aeroplane Experimental Establishment (AEE) at Martlesham Heath in Suffolk, it was found to be difficult to control while landing and to be of 'flimsy' structure. The second, J6898, was stronger and undertook full load trials at the AEE in early 1924, but entered storage at Farnborough, Hampshire, by the end of March, destined never to fly again. The RAF selected the Vickers Victoria to fulfil Specification 5/20.

VICKERS VICTORIA

The Victoria was a troop-carrying version of the Virginia bomber with a new fuselage, the first of two prototypes flying on 22 August 1922. A total of 94 Victorias were produced for the RAF by December 1933, the first nine as Mk IIIs with wooden structure, which was replaced by metal in the main production variant, the Mk V. The 11 new-build Victoria VIs had Bristol Pegasus IM3 engines in place of the Napier Lions of the earlier aircraft, 23 of which were upgraded to the latter standard. The Victoria VI was an interim model. In order to take full advantage of the greater power available from the Pegasus, Vickers strengthened the airframe, incorporated a strut rather than wire-braced landing gear, added wheel brakes and replaced the tail skid with a wheel. Aircraft with these changes became Valentia Is, of which 28 were built and 54 were converted Victorias. Most Victorias and Valentias served with the RAF overseas. This aircraft is the first Victoria VI built, delivered in late 1933. Its entire service career was spent with 70 Squadron at Hinaidi in Iraq, the aircraft becoming a Valentia I in late 1935. It was destroyed by fire on 4 April 1936, after being hit by a flare.

BRISTOL TRAMP

During the 1920s, the British aviation industry produced large number of aircraft only as prototypes – some never even made it to a maiden flight. The Bristol Type 37 Tramp was designed for the RAF as a 'spares carrier', initially to Specification DofR (Directorate of Research) Type 11 and later Specification 1/20 within the new Directorate of Technical Development series. It was conceived as a variant of the Type 33 Pullman passenger transport. One of its unusual features was the use of four 230hp (172kW) Siddeley Pumas, with a pair of the engines turning a single four-blade propeller each side of the fuselage. The Air Ministry placed a contract for two Type 37s, dated 6 October 1921. By the time the first aircraft, J6912, was completed, persistent problems with the transmission system had ended RAF interest in the aircraft. All work had ceased on the aircraft by the time it was transported to the RAE at Farnborough, Hampshire, in October 1922 for use as a ground test rig. There it was joined by the second Tramp in January 1923, which served as a source of spares for the first. Neither aircraft ever flew; J6912 was scrapped in September 1924.

AVRO ALDERSHOT

Roy Chadwick designed the Avro 549 Aldershot three-bay biplane, long range bomber to Specification 2/20. It was the first Avro aircraft with a metal fuselage frame. Prototype Aldershot I J6852 was the first of two powered by the Rolls-Royce Condor III ordered in December 1920. Following evaluation by the AEE in early 1922, a larger rudder was fitted and its fuselage lengthened by 6ft (1.83m). It served as a development aircraft throughout its flying career, mainly with the RAE at Farnborough, testing the 1,000hp (746kW) Napier Cub I from late 1922 as the Aldershot II and the 850hp (634kW) Beardmore Typhoon I (as the Mk IV) during 1927. The main production version for the RAF was the Condor III-powered Aldershot III, which had a stronger undercarriage, a lower fuselage gun position and upper-wing fuel tanks. Fifteen were built (three possibly as Mk Is) and served with 99 Squadron at Bircham Newton, Norfolk, from July 1924 until December 1925, notably helping to develop night bombing tactics. They were replaced by Handley Page Hyderabads, concluding the era of the single-engined heavy bomber in the RAF.

HANDLEY PAGE HYDERABAD

Handley Page adapted its W.8 airliner to create the W.8d (later HP.24) Hyderabad heavy night bomber to satisfy Air Ministry Specification 31/22. Although only 45 were built – including a single prototype – it had the distinction of being the last wooden heavy bomber flown by the RAF. The prototype first flew on 23 October 1923, making its public debut in the New Types Park at the Hendon Air Pageant in north London on 28 June the following year. Early production aircraft began arriving at Bircham Newton, Norfolk, in December 1925 to equip 99 Squadron, the first operational unit. Delivery of Hyderabads was slow and it was more than two years before 10 Squadron became the second unit to receive the bomber on 3 January 1928. Both squadrons were based together at Upper Heyford, as the initial operator had moved to the Oxfordshire airfield in December 1927. Two Special Reserve squadrons, with a mix of regular and reserve personnel, were the only others to fly the aircraft. Between July 1928 and February 1932, 502 (Ulster) Squadron based its bombers at Aldergrove, Northern Ireland. Hyderabads last served with 503 (City of Lincoln) Squadron, which flew them from Waddington, Lincolnshire, until February 1934.

BEARDMORE AV1 INFLEXIBLE

The Inflexible was notable for its size – in its time, it was the largest aircraft to fly – and construction methods. A single aircraft was ordered to Specification 18/23, which outlined an all-metal experimental civil landplane. Construction of the Inflexible began after William Beardmore and Company of Dalmuir, Scotland, concluded an agreement with Rohrbach in 1924, which included a licence for the German company's stressed metal skin construction techniques and the drawings of its Ro VI, from which the Inflexible was developed. The civil registration G-EBNG was reserved for the aircraft but was cancelled before it was completed, by when the military markings J7557 had been allocated. The Inflexible was built in sections that were shipped to Martlesham Heath, Suffolk, for assembly. It first flew on 5 March 1928, in the hands of Jack Noakes. Over the next 20 months, the aircraft was evaluated at the airfield, appearing at the Hendon RAF Display in north London on 27–30 June 1928, with New Types Park identity '9'. The following year, it was displayed at the Norwich Aero Club Display at Mousehold, Norfolk, on 18–20 May and the Cambridge Aero Club Display, Conington, on 10–11 June (as seen here). As no production order was forthcoming, the Roll-Royce Condor II engines were removed in January 1930 and the aircraft was dismantled at Martlesham Heath.

BLACKBURN IRIS

Only five Blackburn Iris flying boats were built. The prototype RB (Reconnaissance Biplane) 1 Iris I first flew from the Humber estuary on 19 June 1926, having been built at Blackburn's Olympia Works in Leeds, Yorkshire. The Iris I was later modified with a metal (in place of the original wooden) hull and more powerful variants of the Rolls-Royce Condor as the RB.IA Iris II. In 1931, it was again re-engined, with Armstrong Siddeley Leopard IIIs, to become the RB.IC Iris IV. The Iris II performed well during a tour around the Baltic in August and September 1927, resulting in the Air Ministry writing Specification R.31/27 for an improved version, leading to delivery of three all-metal RB.IB Iris IIIs with Condor IIIBs to the RAF. They first flew on 21 November 1928, and they entered service with 209 Squadron at Mount Batten, Plymouth, Devon, in January 1930. At the time, they were the RAF's largest aircraft, and they were used on many long-distance flights. After an Iris III was lost in February 1931, an additional aircraft (S1593, seen here) was ordered with a revised bow gun position to accommodate a 37mm (1.5in) Coventry Ordnance Works cannon. It first flew on 25 June 1931. All three surviving Iris IIIs were later upgraded as RB.ID Iris Vs with more powerful Rolls-Royce Buzzard IIMS engines; S1593 flew again following upgrade on 31 March 1933. It was used to test various airscrews before being withdrawn from use in June 1934. In 1937, it was selected as a testbed for the Napier Culverin I diesel engine (a licence-built Junkers Jumo IVC). Returning to the air on 9 June, it only logged 15hrs 35mins before being grounded again.

SUPERMARINE SOUTHAMPTON

Southampton II S1249 is seen with the throttles of its two Napier Lion VAs opened up as it struggles to lift into the air. The Southampton was developed to Specification R.18/24 from the civil Swan, designed by Reginald Joseph Mitchell, and became one of the most successful of the RAF's large biplane flying boats of the interwar period. The first of an initial order for six for the RAF flew on 10 March 1925 and the service eventually purchased 18 Mk Is with wooden hulls and 48 Mk IIs with duralumin units. All surviving Mk Is were upgraded as Mk IIs between 1929 and 1933 and later, after the retrofit of metal wings, some became Mk IIIs. Southamptons entered service with 480 (Coastal Reconnaissance) Flight – later 201 Squadron – at Calshot, Hampshire, in August 1925. From September 1928, 482 Flight operated Southamptons from Mount Batten, Devon, before becoming 203 Squadron and moving to Basra in Iraq. Two other squadrons – 204 and 210 – also flew the flying boat from bases in Britain. On 14 October 1927, four Southamptons of the Far East Flight commenced a 27,000-mile (43,451km) journey from Felixstowe, Suffolk, to their new operating base in Singapore, later visiting Australia and Hong Kong. The Flight became 205 Squadron on 8 January 1929 and had the distinction of operating the last Southamptons in the RAF, withdrawing its final example in February 1936. Southamptons were also exported to Argentina (eight aircraft), Japan (one) and Turkey (six), while two former RAF aircraft were supplied to Australia.

BRISTOL 81A PUMA ADVANCED TRAINER

The Bristol F2b Fighter was one of the great aircraft of World War One and remained in service with the RAF well into the 1920s, with the basic airframe spawning multiple derivatives. The Bristol Type 29 Tourer give rise to the Type 81 Puma School Trainer of 1922, four of which were built for the Filton Reserve Flying School. Six similar aircraft were ordered as 81A Puma Advanced Trainers by the Hellenic Navy, with larger rudders and radios and the provision to be converted to fighters if required. This example is depicted undergoing flight tests with Bristol, with (left to right) Engineer Lieutenant Alifantis, Bristol's Chief Test Pilot Cyril F Uwins and Lieutenant Commander Retsinopoulo beneath the engine. All six were test flown in England during April and May 1925, using a single Armstrong Siddeley Puma engine supplied by the Hellenic Naval Air Service, which was swapped between the aircraft as needed. They were shipped to Greece without engines and had Pumas installed once they arrived. In 1930, the Naval Air Service merged with Hellenic Army Aviation to create the Royal Hellenic Air Force. The Type 81As were transferred to the new service and, in 1931, re-engined with Rolls-Royce Falcons and fitted with a Scarff-type gunner's ring for the rear cockpit. Greece retired the Type 81A in 1935.

ARMSTRONG WHITWORTH SISKIN

The Siddeley-Deasy SR2 Siskin of 1919 was further developed by Armstrong Whitworth as the Siskin II, two of which were built in 1923 with civil markings. Work continued to meet an RAF requirement for an all-metal fighter as the Siskin III, the prototype making its maiden flight on 7 May 1923. A total of 61 were built for the RAF to equip 41 Squadron at Northolt, Middlesex, from May 1924, and from that June, 111 Squadron at Duxford, Cambridgeshire. The Siskin III was replaced in production by the Mk IIIA powered by the more powerful Armstrong Siddeley Jaguar IV instead of the Jaguar III of the earlier variant. The first Siskin IIIA flew on 21 October 1925, and 340 were built by Blackburn, Bristol, Gloster and Vickers, as well as by the parent company, the last of which was delivered in 1931. Siskins IIIAs replaced Mk IIIs with 41 and 111 Squadrons and other types with 1, 17, 19, 25, 29 (seen here), 32, 43, 54 and 56 Squadrons. The last frontline Siskin unit was 56 Squadron at North Weald, Essex, which received Bulldog IIAs in October 1932. The RAF also had dual control trainer versions of both the Siskin III and IIIA. They were issued to Flying Training Schools at Grantham, Lincolnshire; Sealand, Flint; the RAF College at Cranwell, Lincolnshire; and in ones and two to most squadrons with Siskin single-seaters.

HAWKER HORSLEY

Hawker's last aircraft of wooden construction for the RAF was the Horsley I day bomber. The prototype first flew in late 1924. This aircraft, J7721, is the second prototype, which first flew on 6 December 1925, and went to the RAE in June 1926, prior to its performance evaluation at the Aeroplane and Armament Experimental Establishment (A&AEE) at Martlesham Heath, Suffolk, the following month. Hawker switched to a mixture of wooden and metal structures for the Mk II, produced as bombers and torpedo-bombers, after building ten Mk Is. A prototype all-metal Horsley flew around April 1927 and the new construction material was used for a batch of 36 Mk IIs torpedo-bombers for the RAF. A total of 124 Horsleys were built, including six sold to the Hellenic Navy (and two similar Dantorps to Denmark). Two Horsley IIs were modified by the RAF for long-distance flights. At 1038hrs on 20 May 1927, Flight Lieutenants Charles Roderick Carr (pilot) and Leonard Edward Moreland Gillman (observer) departed Cranwell in Lincolnshire in J8607, heading for India. After 34hrs 30mins aloft, they came down in the Persian Gulf, running out of fuel after flying 3,419 miles (5,504km), a record distance. Unfortunately, a few hours later Charles Lindbergh landed at Le Bourget, Paris, at the end of his 3,609-mile (5,809km) transatlantic flight.

BLACKBURN TR1 SPRAT

A two-seat, advanced trainer with interchangeable float or wheel landing gear, the Blackburn Sprat was produced in response to a 1926 Air Ministry specification and based on the earlier Dart and Swift. It was intended to bridge the gap between the Avro 504 primary trainer and various frontline aircraft. Power was provided by a 270hp (201kW) Rolls-Royce Falcon III, also used by the competing designs produced by Parnall and Vickers, the Perch and Vendace. Only one Sprat was built (N207). An unusual feature was the instrument panel, which was attached to the upper wing trailing edge, so it could be seen by both pupil and instructor in the tandem cockpits. Flight Lieutenant 'George' Paul Ward Spencer Bulman took the Sprat aloft for its first flight on 24 April 1926, after which it went to the A&AEE at Martlesham Heath for evaluation as a landplane. Trials with floats followed at the Marine Aircraft Experimental Establishment (MAEE) at Felixstowe, also in Suffolk. It reverted to wheels for its public debut as 'No 2' in the New Types Park at the Hendon RAF Display on 3 July 1926, by when the rival Vendace had been selected, although the requirement was soon abandoned.

PARNALL PETO

Admiralty interest in aircraft-carrying submarines reached its zenith in the late-1920s. Specification 16/24 outlined a 'two-seat float seaplane for storage in a restricted space' that could be housed in space formerly occupied by a 12in (30.5cm) gun on the submarine HMS *M2*. Initially, it was expected the aircraft would be lowered onto the sea to take off and scout ahead of the submarine, after which it would land alongside to be hoisted on board. Parnall built two prototype Petos, a compact biplane with folding wings, to the specification. Peto N181 first flew 4 June 1925, powered by a Lucifer IV, later replaced by a Mongoose IIIC. The second aircraft, N182, flew in the summer of 1926 and, by July, had undergone evaluation at Felixstowe, Suffolk. During 1927, *M2* was equipped with a hangar and, in October 1928, it was further modified with a hydraulic catapult so it could launch the aircraft (rather than take off from the sea). The first Peto was badly damaged during service trials in Gibraltar on 11 February 1930 but was rebuilt with metal (rather than wooden) floats and new wings, becoming N255. It was embarked on *M2* when the submarine sank on 26 January 1932 in West Bay, off Portland, Dorset, with the loss of all 60 on board. The second Peto crashed at Stokes Bay, off Hampshire, on 29 June 1930 and, although the wreck was sold to a private owner, it never flew again.

GLOSTER IV

In early 1926, the Gloster Aircraft Company began work on a new floatplane racer for the Schneider seaplane race to be held at Venice the following year. Using the earlier Gloster III as a starting point, designer Henry Philip Folland created a biplane that was around 70mph (113km/h) faster by improving the aerodynamics and using a more powerful Napier Lion VII engine. Three aircraft were ordered as N222 to N224 as the Gloster IVA, IVB (seen here) and IV respectively, with slight differences. The IVB (and IVA) had a smaller wing area than the IV and was powered by a geared Lion VIIB (rather than direct drive VIIA) driving a 7ft 8.5in (2.35m) propeller. All three were delivered to Calshot, Hampshire, in July and August 1927, before N222 and N223 were shipped to Venice. On 21 September, during a practice run for the race, N223 lost its spinner and damaged a propeller blade, but was quickly repaired. Five days later at the race, Flight Lieutenant Samuel Marcus Kinkead in N223 (race number '1') achieved 277.1mph (445.9km/h) – a record still for biplane seaplanes – on his third lap. The Gloster IVB slowed for the fourth lap and further still on its fifth, prompting Kinkead to retire from the contest. It was found that the propeller shaft had cracked three-quarters of the way around its diameter – Kinkead's decision to withdraw probably saved his life. Both N222 and N223 were later modified as trainers for the British Schneider team. On 19 December 1930, Flight Lieutenant John Boothman crashed and destroyed N223 while landing in fog; Boothman went on to win the Schneider Trophy outright for Britain in 1931.

SUPERMARINE S.6

For the 1929 Schneider Trophy contest, the High Speed Flight at Felixstowe, Suffolk, had two Supermarine S.6 and two Gloster VI racing floatplanes. The S.6 was a development of the earlier S.5 with a specially designed, larger, and more powerful Rolls-Royce powerplant. Held at Spithead off Calshot, Hampshire, on 6–7 September, the two S.6s were triumphant, with Flying Officer Henry Richard Danvers Waghorn winning with an average speed of 328.63mph (528.86km/h). The S.6s were later flown by Flying Officer Richard Llewellyn Roger Atcherley to raise the speed records over courses of 50km and 100km (31 and 62 miles) to 332mph and 331mph (534 and 532.6km/h). Both aircraft were later fitted with new, larger floats as S.6As, and while one (N248, '4', in the middle) was part of the team for the 1931 contest the main hope rested on the two S.6Bs (S1595 '1' and S1596 '7'). The S.6Bs were powered by the 2,300hp (1,716kW) Rolls-Royce R and had larger floats, the upper portion of which, as well as the whole of the wing surfaces, housed radiators for the power plant. On 13 September, Flight Lieutenant John Nelson Boothman came first at the 1931 Schneider contest in S.6B S1595, with an average speed of 340.08mph (547.29km/h), winning the Trophy outright for Great Britain. Seventeen days later, Flight Lieutenant George Hedley Stainforth broke the 400mph (644kmh) speed barrier for the first time, raising the world speed record to 407.5mph (655.8km/h).

ARMSTRONG WHITWORTH ATLAS

First flown on 10 May 1925, the Armstrong Whitworth Atlas was a private venture designed to Specification 33/26 for a two-seat army co-operation aircraft. Production totalled 478, of which 446 went to the RAF, either as army co-operation aircraft or dual-control trainers. They entered RAF service in October 1927 with 26 Squadron at Catterick, Yorkshire, and went on to equip 2, 4, 13, 16 and 208 Squadrons, the last based at Heliopolis in Egypt, and the others at home bases. The 175 unarmed dual-control Atlases became standard equipment at Flying Training Schools based at Digby, Lincolnshire; Netheravon, Wiltshire; Sealand, Flint; and Grantham, Lincolnshire, as well as in Egypt and with the RAF College at Cranwell, Lincolnshire. Atlas trainers were replaced by Hawker Hart Trainers from 1935, the army co-operation aircraft having been superseded by Hawker Audaxes in the early 1930s. A single Atlas (J9998) served as a floatplane trainer for pilots flying the Schneider Trophy racers. It was fitted with stainless steel floats and a 560hp (418kW) Armstrong Siddeley Panther VI in place of the standard 400hp (298kW) Armstrong Siddeley Jaguar IVC, to improve performance and overcome water resistance during take-off. The aircraft was operated by the High Speed Flight at Calshot, Hampshire, from June 1931.

BOULTON & PAUL P.29 SIDESTRAND

Two prototype Sidestrand medium day bombers were built to Specification 9/24, the first flying in the late summer of 1926. Powered by a pair of 425hp (317kW) Bristol Jupiter VIs, the Sidestrand demonstrated remarkable manoeuvrability for its size, as pilots found they could loop, roll and spin it without difficulty. A total of six Mk IIs with ungeared Jupiter VIs and 13 Mk IIIs with geared Jupiter VIIIFs were built for the RAF, the earlier aircraft being upgraded to the later standard after delivery. Only 101 Squadron ever flew the Sidestrand, based at Bircham Newton, Norfolk, between March 1929 and July 1936, receiving the similar Overstrand (originally designed as the Sidestrand Mk IV) from January 1935. With its Sidestrands, the squadron built up a good reputation for bombing accuracy over the ranges, while it also regularly demonstrated the aircraft at the annual air pageants held at Hendon in north London. Sidestrand 'G', J9769, was built as a Mk III and served with 101 Squadron from April 1931 until it was destroyed in a ground taxiing accident in November 1932.

HAWKER TOMTIT

The seventh Hawker Tomtit, J9777, taking off from Brooklands, Surrey, for delivery to the RAF in October 1929. It went to the Central Flying School, quickly passing to 3 Flying Training School at Grantham, Lincolnshire. Its flying career was short, as on 14 July 1930, it collided with Armstrong Whitworth Siskin IIIA(DC) J9190 while attempting to take off. Leading Aircraftman Edwin James Palmer flying the Siskin was killed, but Pilot Officer Derek Harcourt Oxley in the Tomtit suffered only slight injuries, although his aircraft was written off. Originally designed to replace the Avro 504N as the RAF's standard elementary trainer, the all-metal Tomtit had several sophisticated features, such as the Reid and Sigrist blind flying panel, but was expensive to purchase. In November 1928, Paul Ward Spencer Bulman – known as George – flew the Tomtit prototype for its first flight at Brooklands, Surrey, with the aircraft later going to the Air Ministry as J9772. An initial order for ten for the RAF (including J9777) was placed in March 1929, followed by a further six in July 1930 and eight in January 1931. They were declared obsolete by the RAF in 1935. A further five Tomtits were built for private owners, while two went to Canada and four to New Zealand.

CHAPTER 5

THE 1930S
WINGS OF PEACE

Technological developments enabled commercial operators to set their sights on destinations considerably further afield. Passenger and mail transport routes were established across the British Empire, while a new generation of light aircraft catered to the needs of the private flyer. The 1930s was a golden age for British civil aviation. Rapid advances in technology created safer aircraft with better performance, flying faster, higher and further. Open cockpits gave way to cabin aircraft, providing some protection against the cold and weather. Outside the confines of the official specifications that outlined military requirements and airliners for the state-sponsored carriers, designers had a free reign to create aircraft that pushed technology and performance boundaries to offer to the private operator or owner. These gave rise to a generation of 'gentlemen's air carriages' for those with the means. Many of these were monoplanes at a time when the standard fighter in the RAF was a biplane. Learning to fly at the local airfield became a fashionable thing to do. Air races and competitions were common and attracted large crowds, while the exploits of notable pilots were reported in the broadsheets. Inspired by the high levels of 'air mindedness' in the country at the time, many municipal authorities became determined to build and operate their own aerodromes, several of which only opened in time to play a role in World War Two.

ROYAL AIRSHIPS WORKS R101

In 1929, the British government sponsored two civil airships for use on routes within the Empire under the Imperial Airship Scheme. A subsidiary of Vickers-Armstrong was responsible for the R100, its design team headed by Barnes Wallis. The R101 was designed and built by the Royal Airship Works, an Air Ministry team, at Cardington, Bedfordshire. It was the largest aircraft ever constructed in Britain and was only exceeded in length by the later German *Hindenberg* and *Graf Zeppelin II*. After inflating the gasbags with hydrogen on 21 September 1929, it was discovered that the structural weight was above estimates and the lift from the gas was lower than expected. The airship was also tail-heavy. On 12 October, the R101 was walked out of its shed by a ground crew of 400. Two days later, it made its maiden flight, passing over Bedford and London before returning to Cardington. Subsequent flights were a mix of development sorties and public relations work for the airship programme, during which the R101 suffered from tearing of its exterior fabric and gas leaks, which compounded its lack of lift. On 29 June 1930, work began adding additional gasbags to increase lift, requiring the hull to be lengthened to 777ft (236.80m). The R101 flew again on 1 October and, three days later, it departed Cardington for Karachi, then in India, carrying dignitaries and officials from the Royal Airships Works. The weather deteriorated before crossing the English Channel and the R101 came down on 5 October at Allonne, southeast of Beauvais, France. Of the 54 on board, 48 were killed, including Lord Thompson, who was in charge of the airship programme, and most of the R101's designers.

HANDLEY PAGE HP.42

Few aircraft are as closely associated with the glamour of air travel in the 1930s as the Handley Page HP.42/45, the largest airliner in regular use when it entered service. The HP.42 and HP.45 were designed for Imperial Airways, the former for routes from Africa and India and the latter on European services. Each had two cabins, which in the HP.42 accommodated six (later increased to 12) and 12 passengers, respectively, in considerable luxury, plus substantial baggage space. Squadron Leader Thomas Harold England made the maiden flight in HP.42 G-AAGX on 14 November 1930. All HP.42/45s were named after historic figures with names beginning with 'H': G-AAGX was *Hannibal* and the other HP.42s were *Hecate* (later *Horsa*), *Hanno* and *Hadrian*. *Hannibal* suffered a forced landing at Five Oak Green in Kent on 8 August 1931, following an engine failure. It was repaired at Croydon, London, and returned to service. The HP.45 was configured to carry more passengers with reduced baggage over shorter ranges. Four were delivered as *Heracles*, *Horatius*, *Hesperides* (later *Hengist*) and *Helena*. *Hengist* and *Helena* were later modified to a configuration similar to the HP.42s. By September 1939, four were based at Cairo, Egypt, and three in Britain (*Hengist* having burnt out in May 1937). All seven were lost or withdrawn by the end of 1940, including three impressed into 271 Squadron of the RAF in the middle of the year. *Hannibal* was lost with all eight on board over the Gulf of Oman on 1 March 1940.

ARMSTRONG WHITWORTH AW.XV ATALANTA

The Atalanta was designed in response to an Imperial Airways requirement for an aircraft for its African routes, carrying nine passengers and freight with a crew of three. The prototype, G-ABPI, first flew on 6 June 1932 from Whitley Abbey near Coventry, Warwickshire. Imperial Airways ordered eight, with the prototype, named *Atalanta*, flying the aircraft's initial service from Croydon to Brussels, Belgium, and Cologne, Germany, on 26 September 1932. Once in service, however, Atalantas proved too small to cater for the demand for travel between Kenya and Cape Town, South Africa. They also operated on the route between Karachi and Calcutta in India, which was later extended to Rangoon (Yangon), in Burma, and Singapore. Two were leased to Wilson Airways of Kenya when Imperial Airways withdrew the type from its Africa routes in 1937, operating them until July 1938. Five Atalantas – named *Atalanta, Artemis, Astraea, Arethusa* and *Aurora* – survived to join British Overseas Airways Corporation (BOAC) when it was created in late 1939. They were impressed in March 1941 for use by the RAF in India, before passing to the Indian Air Force for coastal reconnaissance and transport duties. *Atalanta* was destroyed landing at St Thomas' Mount in India on 22 August 1942. The last pair were retired in June 1944.

BOULTON & PAUL P.64 MAILPLANE

Transport of mail was an important stimulus to the development of aviation in the 1920s and 1930s. In the late 1920s, Imperial Airways formulated a requirement for a mailplane that could carry 1,000lb (454kg) over 1,000 miles (1,609km) at a speed of at least 150mph (241km/h), while maintaining a height of 5,000ft (1,524m) with a full load should one engine fail. At least eight companies expressed interest in the requirement, which was outlined in Air Ministry Specification 21/28, with Boulton & Paul of Norwich, Norfolk, and Handley Page submitting tenders. A contract for a single prototype was let to Boulton & Paul for the P.64 Mailplane, an all-metal two-engine biplane transport. It first flew from the company's premises at Mousehold, Norwich (as seen here), in March 1933 as G-ABYK and was sent to Martlesham Heath, Suffolk, for evaluation by the Air Ministry. Alarming yaw characteristics resulted in the addition of auxiliary fins, but during a flight to confirm the modification, the Mailplane dived into the ground on 21 October 1933, injuring Flight Lieutenant Gordon Lennox George Richmond. A lighter, slimmer and longer-range development of the P.64 was produced as the P.71A, with Imperial Airways accepting two in February 1935.

ARMSTRONG WHITWORTH AW.27 ENSIGN

A modern-looking, high-wing monoplane constructed from light alloys, the AW.27 had a retractable landing gear (a novelty at the time) and was powered by four Armstrong Siddeley Tigers. It could accommodate either 40 or 27 (day) or 20 (sleeper) passengers depending on configuration, plus a crew of five. Imperial Airways ordered the first in September 1934, followed by a contract for 11 more in May 1935, and an additional pair during December 1936. Assembly of the prototype (G-ADSR) by Air Service Training at Hamble, Hampshire, advanced so slowly that test pilot Charles Turner-Hughes had to wait until 24 January 1938 to make the type's first flight. At that point, the airliner was the largest landplane flown in Britain. The prototype was named *Ensign* by Imperial Airways and the fleet became the 'Ensign class'. *Ensign* G-ADSR entered service in October 1938, flying between London and Paris, and three others had been delivered before the end of December, although the fleet returned to Armstrong Whitworth for modification the following year. The 11 in service at the outbreak of war passed to BOAC in November 1939 and flew throughout the conflict in civil markings, primarily in the Near East. Eight had their Tigers replaced by Wright Cyclones, which had been installed from the outset in the final two, built in 1941 as Ensign IIs. The survivors were scrapped in 1947.

SHORT EMPIRE

Short S.23 Empire C-Class flying boat *Capella* undergoing an overhaul at Southampton docks, Hampshire, in mid-1937. The aircraft was delivered to Imperial Airways on 16 February 1937. *Capella* hit an unknown object while taxiing in Batavia Harbour at Jakarta in the Dutch East Indies (now Indonesia) on 12 March 1939, while undertaking a service for Qantas. All eight on board got out safely, but the flying boat sank and was damaged beyond repair. *Capella* was one of 42 Empires built. Orders comprised 28 S.23s powered by four Bristol Pegasus XC engines, the first (G-ADHL, *Canopus*) making its maiden flight on 4 July 1936, at the hands of Short's test pilot John Lankester Parker. The aircraft conducted its first service for Imperial Airways on 17 September. Three of the original order were diverted to Qantas. An additional contract for 11 was placed by the British airline in late 1937, including three more S.23s for Qantas, with the rest completed as S.30s with Perseus XIIc engines. A final S.30 was ordered in 1939 and delivered in March 1940. Four S.30s were equipped with in-flight refuelling equipment for the transatlantic mail service. The last order covered three S.33s, with Pegasus engines, only two of which were built.

DE HAVILLAND DH.80A PUSS MOTH

Between 1929 and 1933, de Havilland built 259 DH.80A Puss Moths at Stag Lane in London, plus a further 25 in Canada. The three-seat high-wing design was one of the best-performing aircraft available to the private flyer at the turn of the decade. The prototype DH.80 flew on 9 September 1929, later becoming the DH.80A after the wooden fuselage structure was replaced by fabric covered steel tubing. The first production Puss Moth was active by March 1930, and it quickly accumulated sales. Puss Moth G-ABFY was a 1931 model, displayed on the stand of the French firm Morane-Saulnier at the 1930 Paris Air Show between 28 November and 14 December. It was later sold to a private owner and operated from Castle Bromwich in the West Midlands. During June 1931, Dunlop Rubber used G-ABFY as a test bed for low pressure tyres. On 5 September 1931, the aircraft was registered to Lieutenant Frederick Edward Clifford, who, accompanied by Michael Pearce, departed later that month for Cape Town in South Africa, where the Puss Moth was sold, later finding its way to the Durban Light Plane Club.

ARROW ACTIVE

Arrow Aircraft of Yeadon in Leeds, Yorkshire, designed an attractive single-seat biplane with staggered wings known as the Active. The company hoped the design would be adopted by the military, but it transpired that only two Actives were built. The Active 1 (G-ABIX, in the foreground) was powered by an 115hp (86kW) Cirrus Hermes IIB. It was issued a Certificate of Airworthiness on 21 May 1931. The Active 2 (G-ABVE) differed from its predecessor by having struts between the fuselage and upper wing centre section and a de Havilland Gipsy III engine. Both took part in the 1932 King's Cup Air Race in July at Brooklands, Surrey, finishing in tenth (Active 1) and nineteenth (Active 2) place. The Active 1 was sold to Alex Henshaw in May 1935, but on 30 December that year, it caught fire while he was performing aerobatics, forcing him to take to his parachute. After competing in the 1933 King's Cup Air Race, the Active 2 was put into storage. It was rediscovered at Kirkbymoorside, Yorkshire, in 1957 and rebuilt to airworthy condition by Rollasons at Croydon, London.

DE HAVILLAND DH.83 FOX MOTH

A DH.83 Fox Moth (EC-VVA) was acquired for the Spanish expedition to the River Amazon, led by Captain Francisco Iglesias Brage, a long-distance flyer who had attempted to fly between Spain and Rio de Janeiro, Brazil, in 1929. The aircraft was due to operate from the specially constructed hydrographic ship *Ártabro*, launched in February 1935, which could carry two aircraft with their wings folded in a hangar at the aft of the ship. The Fox Moth was delivered to Spain in early 1934, going to Santa Isabel, in Spanish (later Equatorial) Guinea, that December, where it was fitted with floats and prepared for the expedition. By December 1935, the *Ártabro* was waiting to cross the Atlantic, but the deteriorating situation in Spain resulted in the expedition being cancelled in March 1936. The Fox Moth was returned to Spain and was taken over by the Republicans in July 1936 at the start of the Spanish Civil War. It was captured by the Nationalists in 1939, surviving the conflict to join the post-war Spanish Air Force. In February 1941, the biplane was sold privately as EC-AEI and passed through the hands of several Spanish owners until it was withdrawn in Madrid during early 1959.

AIRSPEED AS.5 COURIER

The AS.5 Courier was a modern, low-wing cantilever monoplane, with a cabin for the pilot and up to five passengers, designed in 1932. Customers had the option of a retractable landing gear – a first for a British production aircraft. One aircraft, G-ACNZ, was acquired by D Napier & Son as a test bed and demonstrator for the company's Rapier IV engine as the sole AS.5C, gaining its Certificate of Airworthiness in June 1934. The following month, Air Vice-Marshal Amyas Eden 'Biffy' Borton flew the aircraft in the King's Cup Race at Hatfield, Hertfordshire, with the race number '37', but was eliminated in the first round. In late 1936, the aircraft was sold to Portsmouth Southsea & Isle of Wight Aviation based at Portsmouth, Dorset, and was later re-engined with an Armstrong Siddeley Lynx IVC, as used by the AS.5A (the two 'B' models having Cheetah Vs), and a fixed landing gear. On 18 March 1940, G-ACNZ was impressed by the Air Ministry as X9346 for use by the Air Transport Auxiliary, serving at White Waltham, Berkshire, and, from June 1940, Hawarden on the Welsh border. In March 1941, it was returned to Airspeed, which used it as a company 'hack'. The Courier was withdrawn to 5 Maintenance Unit in January 1944 and struck off charge three months later. Of the 16 Couriers built, only one, G-ACVF, survived the war to fly again in private hands. It had been withdrawn and scrapped by 1948.

PERCIVAL GULL

Edgar Wikner Percival is seen here flying the prototype D.1 Gull I, the first aircraft designed by the Percival Aircraft Company. The prototype was built by the British Aircraft Company of Maidstone, Kent, and registered to Percival on 7 March 1932, based at Heston in Middlesex. Edgar Percival flew the aircraft in that year's King's Cup Race around Britain on 8-9 July, with the race number '50', recording an average speed of 143mph (237km/h). Soon after, it was badly damaged in a crash, but had been repaired by September 1932, appearing at several races and meetings later that year. In 1933, the original solid canopy hood was replaced by a glazed unit, and a Napier Javelin III engine supplanted the original Cirrus Hermes IV, giving it a top speed above that of many fighters of the day. In July 1935, G-ABUR was sold to Man Mohan Singh, who had become famous as the first Indian pilot to fly solo between England and India. The Gull I was written off on 8 August 1935, at Luwinga in Northern Rhodesia (now in Zambia). A total of 47 production D.2 Gull Fours (Mk II, IIA, IIB and III) and D.3 Gull Sixes were built by 1939.

BRITISH KLEMM BK-1 EAGLE

The British Klemm Aeroplane Company was established to build a licenced copy of the German Klemm L.25 light aircraft as the Swallow at premises at Hanworth in west London. George Harris Handasyde, the company's chief designer and previously with Martinsyde, created the BK-1 Eagle as British Klemm's second product. A clean, low-wing cabin monoplane with a manually retracted landing gear, the Eagle could accommodate two passengers side-by-side behind the pilot. Eagle 1 prototype G-ACRG was registered to the manufacturer on 6 July 1934 and resided at Hanworth throughout its existence, passing through the hands of three owners. The aircraft was written off in June 1938. Five other Eagle 1s were built, one of which was sold to a customer in Portuguese East Africa (Mozambique) and two to Australia. British Klemm became the British Aircraft Manufacturing Co in 1935, building a refined version of the aircraft as the Eagle 2 with a more angular rudder, deeper rear fuselage and modified cockpit doors. A total of 37 Eagle 2s were built.

AIRSPEED AS.6 ENVOY

Prototype AS.6 Envoy G-ACMT is seen flying close to the company's facility near Portsmouth, Dorset, in the second half of 1934. Airspeed test pilot Flight Lieutenant Cyril Henry Arthur Colman had undertaken the maiden flight of the aircraft on 26 June that year, powered by a pair of Wolseley AR.9 Mk IIs. It was later fitted with Wolseley Scorpio I engines and further modified to Envoy Srs II standard with split flaps in early 1936, prior to being sold to Rollason Aircraft Services of Croydon in London. The aircraft was quickly purchased for the Spanish Republicans at the start of the Spanish Civil War, who replaced its original wings with those of AS.6J Envoy Srs II G-AEBV at Barcelona, Spain, with the aircraft also gaining its Cheetah IX engines as a bonus. In late September 1936, the Envoy was delivered to the Nationalists by a Republican defector. It became the personal aircraft of General Mola (known as the 'Director'), one of the three leaders of the Nationalist coup of July 1936 that marked the start of the civil war. On 3 June 1937, the Envoy crashed into high ground near Burgos in an accident that claimed Mola's life. Airspeed built 52 Envoys in three distinct series (to ten different standards) before switching production to the similar Oxford military trainer. A further 11 were assembled by Mitsubishi as the Hinz-Yuru ('young crane') for Japan Air Transport.

DE HAVILLAND DH.89 DRAGON RAPIDE

Effectively a smaller version of the four-engine de Havilland DH.86 Express, the Dragon Rapide found favour with 'regional' airlines in the second half of the 1930s. The prototype first flew on 17 April 1934. A typical pre-war operator was Olley Air Service, founded in January 1934 at Croydon, expanding from charter to schedule services after acquiring several other airlines in the mid-1930s. Olley received G-ACYR, the eleventh Dragon Rapide, direct from de Havilland in February 1935. In July 1936, it was used to transport General Francisco Franco, the leader of the Spanish Nationalists, from the Canary Islands to Spanish Morocco at the start of the civil war, the aircraft returning to Britain in mid-August. During World War Two, Olley's services were administrated by the Associated Airways Joint Committee, but, by the end of the conflict, the Rapide was with Miles Aircraft. It was registered to Reid & Sigrist at Desford, Leicestershire, for a year from August 1947, before entering storage. In 1950, it was sold to Air Couriers, which specialised in converting Dominies (the military variant of the Rapide) and Avro Ansons to civil configurations and was roaded to Croydon. The airframe was later donated to the Spanish dictator General Franco; as of 2021, it was on display at the Museo del Aire at Cuatro Vientos, outside Madrid.

DE HAVILLAND DH.88 COMET

In 1933, Australian Macpherson Robertson offered a £15,000 prize for an air race between Britain and Australia to celebrate the centenary of the State of Victoria the following year. Noting the lack of a suitable British mount for the MacRobertson Air Race, Geoffrey de Havilland tasked his company to design and build an aircraft to win it. The result was the sleek de Havilland DH.88 Comet, three of which were ordered by MacRobertson participants, the first (E-1, later G-ASCP) flying on 8 September 1934 – just six weeks before the race. The 20 competitors departed Mildenhall, Suffolk, on 20 October 1934. *Black Magic* (G-ASCP) flown by Jim and Amy (née Johnson) Mollison was forced to retire at Allahabad in India, after landing with one engine inoperative. Owen Cathcart Jones and Ken Waller in G-ACSR completed the race in fourth place. The winners were Flight Lieutenant Charles William Anderson Scott and Captain Tom Campbell Black in Comet *Grosvenor House* (G-ACSS), who crossed the Flemington Racecourse finish line in Melbourne at 1533hrs on 23 October, with an official flight time of 70hrs, 54mins and 18secs. *Black Magic* later went to Portugal as CS-AAJ *Salazar*, for a flight between Lisbon and Rio de Janeiro, Brazil. The attempt had to be abandoned when the Comet was damaged taking off from Sintra. On 26 February 1935, Carlos Bleck and Costa Macedo made a record flight in *Salazar* between London and Lisbon of 6hrs 30mins. In July 1937, Bleck again used *Salazar* to break his own record by more than an hour.

HAFNER AR.III

During the early 1930s, Austrian rotary-wing pioneers, Raoul Hafner and Bruno Nagler, seeking to design a practical helicopter, perfected a new rotor hub, known as the 'spider web hub', which combined cyclic and collective pitch control in one unit. Hafner decided to use it in an autogyro and moved to Britain after securing financial backing for the project. The AR.III (G-ADMV) was built in 1935 at the Martin-Baker factory at Denham, Buckinghamshire, and test pilot Valentine Henry Baker – the Baker in Martin-Baker – made its first flight that September at Heston, Middlesex. Hafner appointed Arthur Edmond Clouston, a civilian test pilot at Farnborough, Hampshire, to demonstrate the AR.III, which was notable for its ease of control and ability to perform 'jump take-offs'. After a landing accident at Farnborough, the original Pobjoy Cataract engine in the nose was replaced by a Pobjoy Niagara III to create the AR.III Mk 2, which flew again in February 1937. The Admiralty became interested in Hafner's autogyro and orders for an AR.IV and AR.V were placed with Short in January 1940, but work ended when Hafner, labelled a citizen of an enemy country because of the war, was interned that May. The AR.III last flew in mid-1941.

SLINGSBY KIRBY GULL

Frederick Nicholas Slingsby became a founding member of the Scarborough Gliding Club in Yorkshire in the early 1930s. He acquired a set of plans for the German Falke and built the glider in a small woodworking and furniture workshop in Scarborough he held a partnership in. He was soon asked to build a second and, as other orders were received, new premises were found at Kirkbymoorside in September 1934. The Type 12 Kirby Gull was introduced in 1938, available for £188, the prototype flying early that year. A single-seat wooden sailplane with a distinctive gull-shaped wing, nine Kirby Gulls (later Gull 1) were built by Slingsby before the war, while another was produced from plans in New York. Geoffrey Stephenson became the first person to cross the English Channel in a glider using only 'natural lift' (rather than an aerotow) flying a Type 12 known as the 'Blue Gull'. His flight, on 22 April 1939, started with a winch launch from Dunstable, Bedfordshire, and, just over 2hrs 35mins later, he landed in a field outside St Omer in France. Prototypes of the Type 14 Gull 2 side-by-side and 'Cantilever Gull' (Type 15 Gull 3) high performance sailplanes flew in 1940, but the war ended plans for production. The post-war Type 25 Gull 4 was a completely new design.

CHAPTER 6

THE 1930S
THE YEARS OF MILITARY EXPANSION

The RAF was still in its infancy at the end of World War One, but as the decade progressed, and with one eye on the shifting political sands worldwide, the British government increasingly turned to the skies for the nation's protection. Significant military and political developments in Europe and the Far East forced the British government to finally abandon its 'ten-year rule' in March 1932. The relative decline of the Royal Navy – Great Britain's first line of defence – increasing nationalism and the growth of military forces in Europe, plus the nomination of Adolf Hitler to become German's chancellor in January 1933, raised questions about the state of Imperial defence. In addition, Japan's rise as a major military power threatened British interests in the Far East. In early 1934, the government announced it intended to maintain 'parity' with Germany in the air, having previously based its requirements on the size of the French air force. RAF Expansion Scheme A was announced by the government on 18 July 1934, as part of a wider effort to bolster the country's armed services, and was the first of a succession of plans to increase the quantity – and later quality – of the RAF. In 1934, the RAF had around 800 aircraft in 42 frontline squadrons based in the British Isles. By 1939, this had increased to 3,700 aircraft in 157 squadrons, plus considerable reserves.

BRISTOL BULLDOG IIA

The Bulldog was the most widely used RAF single-seat fighter of the early 1930s. The Bulldog I first flew on 17 May 1927 and was selected for production in response to Specification F.9/26 in its Mk II form, the first of which was flown on 21 January 1928. Ten squadrons re-equipped with the Bulldog II/IIA, the latter variant having a strengthened structure, a higher loaded weight and a wider undercarriage with larger tyres. The only other production variant for the RAF was the Type 124 Bulldog TM, a two-seat dual-control trainer used between 1932 and 1935 by the Central Flying School, RAF College and four Flying Training Schools in England and Egypt. Apart from the trainers, the only RAF Bulldogs to serve overseas were those of 3 Squadron, deployed to Sudan during the Abyssinian Crisis – the brutal Italian invasion of Ethiopia – from October 1935 to August 1936. Bulldog IIA K1085 was one of a batch of 23 delivered between January and May 1930. It served with 17 Squadron and was one of three that crashed into trees on a hillside after descending in clouds and mist at Arundel Park, Sussex, on 20 October 1930.

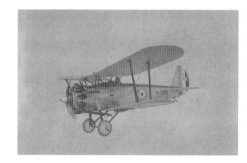

FAIREY IIIF

Fairey IIIF Mk IVM J9172 here heads a line-up of 207 Squadron's machines, possibly at Bircham Newton in Norfolk in late 1931/early 1932. The first Fairey IIIF, developed from the IIID, made its maiden flight on 19 March 1926 and more than 560 were delivered to the RAF and Fleet Air Arm. The first RAF unit with the new variant was 47 Squadron at Khartoum in Sudan in 1927, while 207 Squadron (originally at Eastchurch, Kent) became the initial recipient in Britain. This aircraft was taken on charge by the RAF on 5 October 1928, but, later that year, it was loaned to the Royal Canadian Air Force for cold weather trials as a floatplane at Victoria Beach, Lake Winnipeg, Manitoba. It had returned to Britain by the end of November 1930 and joined 207 Squadron as 'B2' one year later. Its time with the unit was relatively short, as, by September 1932, it was at the Home Aircraft Depot at Henlow, Bedfordshire, for overhaul and modification as a Gordon, returning to the RAF in April 1934. By December 1935, J9172 was serving as a target-tug at Aboukir in Egypt.

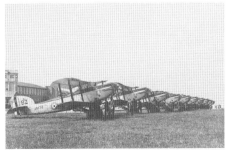

HAWKER YUGOSLAV FURY

In addition to serving as a standard fighter with the RAF, the Fury was sold to several overseas customers. Yugoslavia ordered the Hawker Fury fighter in 1931, before the prototype flew. It commissioned six Series IAs for the Royal Yugoslav Air Force, the first of which flew on 4 April 1931. All but one was fitted with a 525hp (391kW) Rolls-Royce Merlin IIS engine, the exception having a 500hp (373kW) Hispano-Suiza 12NB fitted for evaluation from 27 August 1931, after which it too had a Merlin installed. The six were delivered in 1932. Towards the end of 1934, Yugoslavia sought to increase the size of its Fury force and investigated the 720hp (537kW) Lorraine Petrel Hfrs engine in the aircraft. While a single Fury returned to Hawker as a test bed for the powerplant, the second batch was delivered with the Rolls-Royce Kestrel XVI instead. An order for ten Series II aircraft was placed in October 1935. They had low drag radiators, provision for four (rather than two) guns, increased fuel, a cantilever landing gear and Dowty internally sprung wheels. The first Yugoslav Series II flew on 14 September 1936, and it proved to be the fastest of all Fury variants. Deliveries by Hawker were completed by June 1937 and licence production in Yugoslavia added another 24 from Ikarus and 16 built by Zmaj.

AVRO 626

The two-seat Avro 621 was built in large numbers as the Trainer and Tutor for the RAF, as well as for the air arms of Denmark, Greece and South Africa, plus commercial customers. A variant of the 621 suitable for a wide range of roles, the Avro 626, was developed in 1930 specifically for the export market, with provision for a third cockpit for a gunner. Avro produced several demonstrators to help market the 626, resulting in sales to Argentina, Austria, Belgium, Brazil, Canada, Chile, China (Kwangsi Provisional Government), Egypt, Estonia, Greece, Ireland, Lithuania and Portugal, while a navigator trainer version, known as the Prefect, was delivered to the RAF and Royal New Zealand Air Force. In 1933, ten Avro 626s were ordered by the British government for the Egyptian Army Air Force. They were powered by a 260hp (194kW) Armstrong Siddeley Cheetah V radial engine, in place of the standard 240hp (179kW) Armstrong Siddeley Lynx IVC. Egyptian pilots conducted familiarisation flights at Lympne in Kent (where this line-up is seen) prior to delivery. The first ten departed England in formation on 18 November 1933 but encountered fog over France resulting in two crashing. A further 16 Egyptian Avro 626s were built in 1934 (one of which was lost before delivery), and a single aircraft was delivered in April 1940. In service, they were used for survey flights and patrols over the Sinai desert against hashish traders.

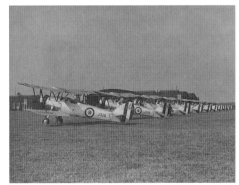

WESTLAND WALLACE

The Wallace was the last of a long line of general-purpose aircraft that served the RAF in the 1920s and 1930s. Designed as the PV.6 private venture by Westland as a development of the earlier Wapiti, it had spatted wheels, a stretched fuselage and the Bristol Pegasus IIM3 in place of the Wapiti's Jupiter, giving it a faster cruise speed. The PV.6 (along with the PV.3) became the first aircraft to fly over Mount Everest on 3 April 1933. A total of 58 Wapitis were converted to Wallace Is for the RAF, of which K3562 was the first. In February 1933, it was produced from Wapiti IIA K1346, which had remained stored at the Home Aircraft Depot since delivery two years earlier. From late 1933, it was evaluated at the Aeroplane and Armament Aircraft Establishment at Martlesham Heath, Suffolk. Wallace Is entered service in January 1933 with 501 'City of Bristol' Squadron, a Special Reserve unit based at Filton, Gloucestershire. The Mk Is were followed by 104 new Mk IIs with the more powerful Pegasus IV engine. In addition to 501, they served with 502, 503 and 504 Squadrons until being replaced in mid 1937. Many were later converted into target-tugs and served with second-line units into 1943; K3562 last flew with the Ground Defence Gunners School until struck off charge in June 1942.

GLOSTER GAUNTLET

The Gauntlet was the last open-cockpit biplane fighter for the RAF. A total of 24 Mk Is and 204 Mk IIs were delivered to the service, the main differences between them being the construction of the fuselage and wing spar. In May 1935, 19 Squadron became the first to receive Gauntlets, and the fighter eventually served with 13 fighter squadrons, as well as five Auxiliary Air Force units. These five Gauntlet IIs belonged to 56 Squadron, which re-equipped with the aircraft in May 1936 and relinquished them in July 1937. For two years after its service introduction, the Gauntlet was the fastest fighter in the RAF. Although most had been replaced by the start of World War Two, four Gauntlets were used by 430 Flight in East Africa against Italian forces during September and November 1940, shooting down at least one aircraft on 7 September. Gauntlets were flown by 33 and 112 Squadrons in Egypt from early to mid-1940 and in Palestine by 6 Squadron from August 1939 until April 1940. The final RAF examples were retired from second-line units during 1943.

FAIREY SEAL

During the 1920s and 1930s, many existing designs were upgraded and renamed to meet Air Ministry and Admiralty requirements. The Fairey Seal carrier-borne spotter reconnaissance aircraft was a development of the Fairey IIIF and was initially known as the IIIF Mk VI, the prototype being created from IIIF Mk IIIB S1325, which returned to the air after modification at Hamble, Hampshire, on 11 September 1930. The first of 90 production Seals delivered to the Fleet Air Arm entered service in 1933. Seal K3481, the fifth of the 11 ordered in the first batch, was handed over between December 1932 and February 1933. It served with 820 and 822 Squadrons, 7 Armament Training Station and 2 Air Observers School, ending its flying career in a crash at Usworth, near Sunderland, on 20 May 1939. Seals served with six frontline FAA squadrons, operating from the aircraft carriers *Courageous*, *Eagle*, *Furious*, *Glorious* and *Hermes*. A small number also served with the RAF, primarily as target-tugs, while the type was also exported to Peru, Latvia, Argentina and Chile.

VICKERS VILDEBEEST

The Vildebeest – Vildebeeste until 1934 – was a two-seat torpedo-bomber. Production of the Vildebeest I began in 1932 and 100 Squadron at Donibristle, Fifeshire, was the first to re-equip with the type that November. This aircraft was one of the 30 Vildebeest IIs – with a more powerful Bristol Pegasus engine – delivered between June and August 1933, going to 100 Squadron. The unit deployed to Seletar, in Singapore, that December and the aircraft later passed to 4 Anti-Aircraft Co-operation Unit, initially at the same airfield. It was struck off charge on 30 January 1942, just 16 days before the surrender of the island to Japan. A total of 98 Vildebeest IIIs were built for the RAF, with a redesigned rear cockpit with room for a third crew member, and were initially flown by 22 and 36 Squadrons. The final RAF variant was the two-seat Mk IV (18 built), powered by the Bristol Perseus VIII, the first going to 42 Squadron in March 1937. Around 100 Vildebeests remained in service at the start of the war, by when it had been relegated to second-line roles in the British Isles. Exports comprised 12 Vincent IIIs delivered to New Zealand in 1935, supplemented later by former RAF aircraft. A further 26 were built in Spain and flown by the Republican side during the Civil War.

BLACKBURN SHARK

The Shark was developed from the private venture B.6, the single prototype of which first flew at Brough, Yorkshire, on 24 August 1933. From November 1933, the B.6 was evaluated at Martlesham Heath, Suffolk, resulting in it being selected as a carrier-borne torpedo-bomber for the FAA, the service eventually receiving 238 Sharks of three versions. The Shark I was powered by the 700hp (521kW) Armstrong Siddeley Tiger IV, which was replaced by the 760hp (567kW) Tiger VI in the Mk II, while the Mk III had a glazed cockpit and dual controls. These four Shark IIs belong to 820 Squadron, the first FAA unit to receive the aircraft, having replaced its Fairey Seals in May 1935. It was followed by 820 and 821 Squadrons the following year, but, during 1937, the Shark was replaced by the Fairey Swordfish in frontline units. Some Sharks were converted into target-tugs and remained in use into 1942. Six Shark IIAs were also built for the Portuguese Navy, while nine were delivered to Canada and a further 17 assembled by Boeing Aircraft of Canada at Vancouver, British Colombia.

FAIREY SEAFOX

A light reconnaissance seaplane that could be catapulted from Royal Navy cruisers, the Fairey Seafox had an all-metal structure with a monocoque fuselage and fabric-covered wings. An unusual feature was that the observer's cockpit was enclosed, while the pilot sat in the open. The prototype first flew on 27 May 1936, and the second on 5 November the same year. They were followed by two production batches of 49 and 15 aircraft, delivered from April 1937, all but one as floatplanes. Fairey Seafox I K8575 went to 716 Catapult Flight in 1937 and was still with that unit on 24 May 1939, when the Admiralty regained total control of the FAA from the RAF. In January 1940, the various catapult flights were pooled together as 700 Squadron, which had 11 Seafoxes along with Fairey Swordfish and Supermarine Walruses. Seafoxes were used to spot for the guns of the three Royal Navy cruisers that defeated the German battleship *Admiral Graf Spee* during the Battle of the River Plate on 13 December 1939.

BLACKBURN SKUA

The all-metal Skua introduced several innovations to the FAA when it entered service. It was the first British naval dive-bomber, the first with a retractable landing gear and variable pitch propeller and was the first of the Admiralty's carrier-based aircraft with flaps. Unfortunately, it was obsolete as a fighter by the time it entered service. Two prototypes were ordered, the first flying at Brough, in Yorkshire, on 9 February 1937, making its public debut in the New Types Park at the annual Hendon display in north London on 26 June. A total of 190 production Skuas were ordered before the aircraft had flown. While the prototypes were powered by a Bristol Mercury IX, that engine was reserved for Bristol Blenheims, so production aircraft had the slightly more powerful Bristol Perseus XII. With the new powerplant, the aircraft became the Skua II, all of which were delivered between October 1938 and March 1940. In late 1938, 800 and 803 Squadrons re-equipped with Skuas for service from HMS *Ark Royal*. They were followed by 801 and 806 Squadrons. Skuas from 800 and 803 Squadrons sank the German cruiser *Köningsberg* in Bergen harbour on 10 April 1940. During 1941, they were withdrawn from frontline units and relegated to training and target-towing roles.

SUPERMARINE WALRUS

Walrus L2271 gathers 'speed' – always a relative term for the 'Shagbat' – while taking off from the sea. Designed and originally produced as the Seagull V, the amphibian entered service with the FAA in 1935 in the spotter-reconnaissance role embarked on major warships. Early aircraft had a metal hull that was later replaced by a wooden unit on the production line. Some 740 were built, serving with the Admiralty, RAF, Royal Australian Air Force, Royal Canadian Air Force and Irish Air Corps, plus other armed forces. The Walrus played a significant, if unsung, role during World War Two, notably in the search and rescue (SAR) role with the RAF. It disappeared from British military service quickly after the conflict, although the Argentine Navy continued to fly the type into the late 1950s. L2271 started its career with 712 Squadron, which operated the type between April 1937 and January 1940. The aircraft remained with the Admiralty until transfer to the RAF in February 1944, with which it served with 277 and 278 Squadrons in the SAR role. It was destroyed in a crash off Flamborough Head in Yorkshire on 6 March 1945.

SHORT SINGAPORE

Short's chief test pilot, John Lankester Parker, made the first flight of the S.5 Singapore flying boat, powered by a pair of Rolls-Royce Condor IIIAs, from the River Medway in Kent on 17 August 1926. Only one was built and, as G-EBUP, it was used by Sir Alan Cobham for a survey flight around Africa from mid-November 1927 to June 1928. It was followed by a single S.12 Singapore II, with four engines mounted back-to-back in nacelles between the wings, turning propellers at both ends. It first flew on 27 March 1930 and was the basis of the S.19 Singapore Mk III for the RAF, which had three fins (rather than one) and four Rolls-Royce Kestrel IXs. Four Mk IIIs were ordered to Specification R.3/33 in August 1933 for evaluation by the MAEE at Felixstowe followed by 33 production aircraft, flown by ten squadrons. At the start of World War Two, 19 Singapore IIIs remained operational, including K4577, which was finally struck off charge on 3 January 1940. The aircraft served with 209 Squadron after delivery in April 1935, and later went to 203 Squadron. The last RAF Singapores belonged to 205 Squadron at Seletar, Singapore, with four of its aircraft going to the Royal New Zealand Air Force in Fiji in October 1941.

SAUNDERS-ROE CLOUD

The Saro A.19 Cloud was a 7/8 passenger amphibious flying boat designed for civil operations. The prototype first flew on 15 July 1930 and three more followed for commercial operators. The third Cloud became the military prototype delivered to the RAF as K2681. Sixteen A.29 Clouds came next, acquired in three batches and equipped as pilot trainers with dual controls and cabins configured for six navigation or radio trainees. Up to 200lb (91kg) of bombs could be carried under the wings and Lewis guns were mounted in the bow and amidships. The first Cloud entered RAF service in August 1933 with 'B' Flight of the Seaplane Training Squadron at Calshot, Hampshire, the intermediate seaplane section of the unit. This aircraft (K2897) was delivered on 19 May 1933, going to 'B' Flight, which displayed four Clouds at the Hendon Pageant in north London in 1936 (as seen here). On 8 January 1937, it nosed over while taxiing on the slipway at Calshot, damaging its bow and undersides beyond economic repair. It became a ground instructional airframe as 938M. Clouds last served with the RAF with 9 Elementary & Reserve Flying Training School at Antsy, Warwickshire, but they had been withdrawn by the start of the war.

SUPERMARINE STRANRAER

The last of Supermarine's big flying boats, the Stranraer was originally known as the Southampton V, although it was more closely related to the Scapa than the earlier design. It was created in response to Specification R.24/31, which called for a twin-engine general-purpose coastal reconnaissance flying boat. The prototype, K3973, first flew on 24 July 1934 and was delivered to the RAF that October for evaluation by the MAEE. It was later used by 210 Squadron before returning to the MAEE and was struck off charge at the end of October 1938. While the prototype was powered by Pegasus IIIM engines with two-blade wooden propellers, production aircraft had the Pegasus Xs turning three-blade metal units. An initial order for 17 was signed in August 1935 and delivered over two years from April 1937, but a second contract for six was cancelled. Stranraers were primarily operated by 228 (April 1937 to April 1939), 209 (November 1938 to April 1940) and 240 (June 1940 to January 1941) Squadrons but did not find favour with their flight crews, who considered the aircraft to be under-powered. A further 40 were built by Canadian Vickers (like Supermarine, a subsidiary of Vickers-Armstrong) for the Royal Canadian Air Force, undertaking coastal reconnaissance patrols until April 1944 and retired in 1946.

HANDLEY PAGE HEYFORD

The last of the RAF's biplane heavy bombers, the Heyford was designed to Specification 23/32. The HP.38 prototype first flew in June 1930 and was followed by 124 HP.50s built to Specification B.19/27 from June 1933. These comprised 14 Heyford Is – K3489 seen here was the first – 22 Mk IAs, 16 Mk IIs and 70 Mk IIIs, the last being completed in July 1936. In November 1933, 99 Squadron at Upper Heyford, Oxfordshire, became the first to be supplied with the bomber and was followed by 7, 9, 10, 38, 78, 97, 102, 148, 149 and 166 Squadrons. Its service career was extended by the rapid expansion of the RAF in the 1930s, as additional squadrons were established, with Heyfords transferred from those that had already received more modern equipment. By the outbreak of war, however, only 166 Squadron still flew Heyfords and it soon re-equipped with Armstrong Whitworth Whitley Is. Two bombing schools continued to fly Heyfords until mid-1940, while a single Mk III was modified by Flight Refuelling Ltd (FRL) for air-to-air refuelling trials. The last handful served as glider-tugs before being withdrawn in July 1941.

BOULTON & PAUL P.75 OVERSTRAND

The Overstrand's claim to fame was that it introduced the enclosed powered gun turret to the RAF. A development of the earlier Sidestrand – it was known as the Sidestrand IV until March 1934 – the bomber had a nose-mounted Boulton & Paul turret with a single Lewis machine gun. More powerful Bristol Pegasus IM.3 engines were installed in place of the Sidestrand's Bristol Jupiters, allowing a heavier bombload to be carried and giving the aircraft a faster cruising speed. The prototype, J9186, seen here, was created by the conversion of a Sidestrand III during 1933. Three more Overstrands were produced by modification, the first arriving at Bircham Newton, Norfolk, on 22 February 1934 for service trials alongside the Sidestrands of 101 Squadron. That squadron was destined to be the only one equipped with the new medium bomber, its first full-service example arriving on 26 February 1935, by when it had moved to Bicester, Oxfordshire. Overstrands initially joined the specially formed 'C' Flight of the squadron, although, by mid-1935, all sections of the unit flew the type. Production of 24 new-build Overstrand Is was completed between October 1935 and July 1936. Front line use was short, however, as, in August 1938, 101 Squadron received Bristol Blenheims. Some Overstrands later served with 2 Air Observers School at Dumfries, Scotland, until July 1940, while one was still flown by the Army Co-operation Development Unit until mid-1941.

ARMSTRONG WHITWORTH AW.23

A single prototype of the Armstrong Whitworth AW.23 was built in response to the Air Ministry's Specification C.26/31 for a dual role bomber-transport, which also spawned the Bristol Bombay and Handley Page HP.51. The AW.23 featured a strong, monoplane wing and retractable landing gear, was powered by a pair of Armstrong Siddeley Tiger VI radial piston engines and armed with turrets in the nose and tail positions, each with a single 0.303in (7.7mm) machine gun. Up to 2,000lb (907kg) of bombs could be carried internally when employed as a bomber, or 24 troops carried when used as a transport. The prototype, K3585, first flew on 4 June 1935, appearing at that year's pageant at Hendon before the end of the month. Arrival for evaluation at Martlesham Heath was delayed until late 1936 because of problems with the Tiger engine, by when the Bombay had been selected for production instead. By early 1937, the prototype had been loaned to FRL for airborne refuelling tests, often acting as the 'tanker', as was the case with the experiments with the Short Empire 'C-Class' flying-boat *Cambria* in 1938. It was registered G-AFRX to FRL in April 1939 and went on to participate in the initial night-time refuelling trials before being destroyed during a German air raid on Ford in West Sussex on 18 August 1940.

BRISTOL TYPE 130 BOMBAY

The Bombay was the last of the between-the-wars troop-transports that could also be used as a long-range bomber. The prototype, K3583, seen here, was first flown on 23 June 1935 from Filton, Gloucestershire. Production of the Bombay, however, was contracted out to Short Brothers and Harland in Belfast, Northern Ireland, as Bristol was fully occupied building Blenheims. In March 1939, the first of 50 production-standard Bombay Is was ready for delivery, with 216 Squadron based in Egypt becoming the first unit to re-equip with the type that September, followed by 117, 267 and 271 Squadrons at Khartoum, Sudan, Heliopolis, Egypt, and Doncaster, South Yorkshire, respectively. In service, the Bombay was predominantly used as a transport, although occasionally it was employed in its secondary bombing role, most notably against Italian forces in Eritrea and Libya during 1940. Bombays continued to be flown by the RAF until more modern, dedicated transport aircraft arrived in sufficient numbers, the final examples being struck off charge in August 1944 in North Africa.

HANDLEY PAGE HP.54 HARROW

Although it served in frontline squadrons for only two years, the Harrow was the first monoplane flown by many bomber crews. It was a development of the HP.51 troop-carrier modified to fulfil Operational Requirement 27 as a heavy bomber and built to Specification 29/35, with the first flying on 10 October 1936. The first 40 aircraft were powered by 830hp (619kW) Bristol Pegasus Xs as Harrow Is and were followed by the production of 60 Mk IIs with the more powerful Pegasus XX. Five frontline bomber units converted to Harrows in 1937, starting with 214 Squadron in January. Four of the unit's aircraft are seen lifting off from the grass runway at its base at Feltwell, Norfolk, the squadron having moved there from Scampton, Lincolnshire, in April 1937. Harrows also served with 37, 75, 115 and 215 Squadrons, but, by the start of the war, all squadrons had replaced the aircraft with Vickers Wellingtons. Many Harrows were later operated as transports, stripped of armament with a streamlined nose fairing, able to carry up to 20 troops. Unofficially known as 'Sparrows', the transports were flown from 1940 by 1680 Flight, which later became 271 Squadron, and also by the Harrow Ambulance Flight. The last 'Sparrow' was finally retired in May 1945.

VICKERS WELLESLEY

Designed as a private venture general-purpose monoplane, the prototype of what became the Wellesley I bomber first flew on 19 June 1935. In September 1935, the Air Ministry ordered 96 aircraft to Specification 22/35, the contract later being increased to cover 176 aircraft. The first was delivered on 18 March 1937 to Martlesham Heath for service evaluation prior to the bomber entering operational service with 76 Squadron at Finningley, South Yorkshire, on 12 April. Four additional squadrons within Bomber Command (35, 77, 148 and 207) re-equipped with the Wellesley, while the aircraft also entered service with 14, 45, 47 and 223 Squadrons in the Middle East and Africa. Wellesleys were used by the RAF on several pioneering long-distance flights. The Long Range Development Flight had three Wellesleys with additional fuel tanks that were used to break the world record for flight distance between 5 and 8 November 1938, flying 7,162 miles (11,526km) between Ismailia, Egypt, and Darwin, Australia, but one force-landed before it reached Australia. Although replaced as a frontline bomber in Britain by the start of World War Two, Wellesleys were used against Italian forces in the Middle East and East Africa during 1940.

BRISTOL BLENHEIM I

One of the pre-production batch of six Blenheim Is, K7034 was transported to Paris in November 1936 for display at the Grand Salon Aéronautique on trestles with the undercarriage retracted. All markings were removed and its external surfaces polished until they gleamed, while large spinners were fitted on the propellers. In April 1937, the same aircraft arrived at Martlesham Heath for operational and armament trials with the A&AEE, during which alterations were made to the dorsal turret. By mid-1939, the aircraft was with 'D' Flight of the A&AEE, which had the task of developing a Blenheim night fighter, playing the role of target for K7033 equipped with a primitive air-to-air radar. During one of these flights, K7034 lost a propeller, but the pilot managed to safely recover to Martlesham Heath. The following day, the propeller was returned to the airfield by a farmer who found it on his land. Blenheim K7034 ended its days as ground instruction airframe 3241M.

AVRO 671 ROTA

Rota I K4232 is seen here over the site of the cathedral at Old Sarum, Wiltshire, in the summer of 1934. Ten Cierva C.30As were ordered from Avro that year, the company having acquired a licence to produce the autogyro as the Avro 671, and were delivered between June 1934 and May 1935. Within the RAF, they were known as Rota Is. Most were initially issued to the School of Army Co-operation at Old Sarum, where the autogyro's ability to take off in a confined area was of particular interest. As the advantages of using light aircraft to support troops in the field began to gain traction, interest in the autogyro as a weapon of war waned, resulting in the RAF placing its Rotas into storage in 1939. This was not the end for the Rota in RAF service, however, as the survivors of the original order and former civilian Avro 671s and C.30As impressed for wartime service were used to calibrate radars. The RAF retired its final examples in late 1945. Rota K4232 was struck off charge in September 1946.

BRISTOL 138A

The Bristol 138A was designed as a high-altitude research aircraft in response to Specification 2/34. It was first flown by the manufacturer's chief test pilot Cyril Uwins on 11 May 1936, powered by a Bristol Pegasus IV with a three-blade propeller. After it was delivered to the RAE at Farnborough, a Pegasus PE.VIS engine with a two-stage supercharger and four-blade propeller was installed. The low pressure at the altitudes the aircraft was designed to operate required special protection for the pilot, including a pressure helmet created by Siebe, Gorman and Co. Squadron Leader Francis Ronald Downs Swain made the first high-altitude flight on 28 September 1936, reaching the record height of 49,967ft (15,230m). On 30 June 1937, Flight Lieutenant Maurice James Adam raised the world altitude record to 53,937ft (16,440m) during a 2hr 15min-flight from Farnborough, during which the aircraft's canopy cracked, although Adam managed to land safely. The RAE continued to operate the Bristol 138A on research flights, but no further record attempts were made. After being withdrawn from use, the aircraft went to Kirkham, Lancashire, in June 1940, where it served as a ground instructional airframe. A second aircraft with two seats, the Bristol 138B (L7037), was ordered in 1935. It was planned to install a Rolls-Royce Kestrel S in the 138B, but although the airframe was delivered to Farnborough in 1937, the powerplant was not, and it never flew.

AIRSPEED AS.30 QUEEN WASP

The Queen Wasp was designed as a gunnery target – although many thought it was too good-looking an aircraft to be shot down. Only two prototypes and five production aircraft were completed. This is the second prototype, K8888, which made its first flight around October 1937 as a floatplane from the waters off Lee-on-Solent, Hampshire, before embarking on HMS *Pegasus* for catapult trials. In December 1937, it went to the MAEE for performance trials, before receiving a standard landing gear for evaluation by the RAE in April 1938. At the end of 1940, it joined the Pilotless Aircraft Unit at St Athan in Wales, which was equipped with de Havilland Queen Bees, the target drone version of the Tiger Moth. This Queen Wasp was badly damaged in a crash on 20 March 1941 but was rebuilt over the following year, finally ending its flying career on 7 July 1943, after another accident inflicted more serious damage. All surviving Queen Wasps were struck off charge by the RAF on 27 July 1943.

AIRSPEED AS.10 OXFORD

A flight of three Oxford Is – including one with a gun turret – of II Flying Training School based at Wittering, Northamptonshire, is airborne in March 1938. The three aircraft were among the first of their type delivered to the RAF; only the furthest away, L4541, survived the war, being struck off charge on 20 March 1946. The Oxford was one of the RAF's standard twin-engine trainers, many serving overseas within the schools of the Commonwealth Air Training Scheme. More than 8,000 were built for the RAF by Airspeed at both Portsmouth, Hampshire, and Christchurch, Dorset, plus others were constructed by de Havilland at Hatfield, Hertfordshire; Standard Motors at Coventry, Warwickshire; and Percival Aircraft at Luton, Bedfordshire. The Oxford I was a general-purpose, bombing and gunnery trainer; the Mk II was a pilot, navigator and radio operator trainer. The final variant to enter service was the AS.46 Oxford V, powered by Pratt & Whitney Wasp Junior engines, which was also used as a pilot, navigator and radio operator trainer. The last RAF unit with Oxfords was 10 Advanced Flying Training School at Pershore, Worcestershire, which retired its aircraft in July 1954.

HAWKER HENLEY

Although designed as a light bomber, the Henley entered RAF service as a target-tug. The prototype, K5115, first flew at Brooklands, Surrey, on 10 March 1937, powered by a Rolls-Royce Merlin F, which was replaced by a Mk I by the time it began its official evaluation at Martlesham Heath in January 1938. While it demonstrated good performance and handling, Air Ministry interest in single-engine light bombers had waned, as a new generation of twin-engined aircraft was then under development for the RAF. In 1939, the prototype passed to Rolls-Royce for modification as a test bed for the Vulture engine, before being struck off charge on 23 March 1941. The second prototype, K7554, was modified as the sole Henley II target-tug by Gloster Aircraft, which was sub-contracted to build 200 to a similar standard as Mk IIIs. The first of these entered service with I Anti-Aircraft Co-operation Unit during November 1938, and the last was handed over in September 1940. It was soon discovered that target presentation for air-to-air engagements caused heavy wear on the Merlin. Although the Henley was relegated to supporting ground-based anti-aircraft guns, the bigger sleeves used for this work reduced the speed of the aircraft, causing the Merlin to overheat and eventually fail. By June 1942, fewer than 40 Henleys remained in service, and they were withdrawn as soon as alternative target-tugs became available.

WESTLAND LYSANDER

While the Lysander is best remembered for ferrying secret agents to and from the occupied continent, it was originally designed for army co-operation. The prototype first flew on 15 June 1936, and Lysander Is entered RAF service in May 1938 with 16 Squadron at Old Sarum, Wiltshire (with which these three served), its pilots praising the aircraft's ability to take off and land in short distances. When war was declared, four Lysander squadrons were initially dispatched to France as part of the British Expeditionary Forces, with others following (including 16 Squadron in April 1940). When Germany launched its western offensive on 10 May 1940, it quickly became apparent that the large and unwieldy Lysander was easy prey for the Luftwaffe's fighters. Combat experience also highlighted the limited utility of the army co-operation squadrons and, after they were withdrawn back across the English Channel, other roles were quickly found for them, until the Lysander could be replaced by single-seat fighter-reconnaissance aircraft. Large numbers of Lysanders were converted for air-sea rescue and target-towing roles, while some Mk III/IIIAs were adapted to support resistance organisations in occupied Europe, carrying additional fuel and a fixed ladder to improve access to the cockpit. The last operational Lysanders belonged to 357 Squadron, a special duties unit active in the Far East until November 1945.

CHAPTER 7

WORLD WAR TWO
QUANTITY AND QUALITY

World War Two dawned after the great advances, both in capability and volume, in aviation during the preceding decade. This progress was made against a backdrop of darkening skies across Europe, and many of the aircraft that we now consider to be iconic made their mark in the battles and skirmishes that followed.

More than 131,000 aircraft were produced in Britain between 1939 and 1945, third only to the United States (303,000) and the Soviet Union (158,000). By the time Britain declared war on Germany on 3 September 1939, the aviation industry had increased output greatly, prompted by successive armament plans formulated during the second half of the 1930s. By 1939, the RAF had a frontline strength of 3,700 aircraft in 157 squadrons, with the last of the biplanes being supplanted by modern monoplanes. The expansion of the front line was supported by investment in the aviation industry that permitted rates of production to increase further, such as the implementation of the Shadow Scheme, which co-opted the automobile industry to initially produce components for, and later assemble, whole aircraft. At the start of 1939, more than 450 aircraft a month were delivered to the British services, increasing to approximately 700 by the middle of the year. During May 1940, the Ministry of Aircraft Production was established under Lord Beaverbrook, permitting the government to control planning and allocate resources to the industry. At its peak of production in 1944, an average of 2,200 aircraft were built each month.

HAWKER HURRICANE

Without a doubt, the Hurricane's finest hour was during the Battle of Britain, when it destroyed more enemy aircraft than all other defences combined. By 1943, it was outclassed as a day fighter but remained in widespread service as a fighter-bomber. The Hurricane V was envisaged as a dedicated ground-attack version for service in Burma. It was powered by a Merlin 32 engine with a four-blade propeller, the most powerful version of the engine installed in the aircraft, restoring performance lost due to weight increases over successive variants. Primary armament was a pair of 40mm (1.5in) Vickers S guns under the wings. Hurricane V KZ193 was a converted Mk IV, one of a batch of 1,455 aircraft delivered from Hawker's facilities at Kingston, Surrey, and Langley, Berkshire, between November 1942 and May 1943. It first flew on 3 April 1943 and is depicted here during a performance test flight with Hawker on 11 August from Brooklands, Surrey. Evaluation of the aircraft by the A&AEE at Boscombe Down, Wiltshire, began in November. During the first half of 1944, KZ193 was with 1 Tactical Exercise Unit at Tealing in Scotland, after which it was shipped to the Far East. It survived the war to be struck off charge on 14 February 1946. Only two other Hurricane Vs were produced: KX405, another converted Mk IV, and NL255, a production prototype. As the Mk V only offered a modest improvement in performance, and large stocks of earlier Hurricane variants were already available in India, production of the Mk V did not go ahead.

FAIREY FULMAR

In 1940, the best fighter available to the FAA was the Fulmar, its first eight-gun carrier-borne aircraft. Designed for a crew of two (to cope with the exacting task of navigating over the sea) and so larger and heavier than land-based fighters, the Fulmar was still a considerable improvement over the Blackburn Skua it replaced. It had the distinction of destroying more enemy aircraft than any other FAA fighter during the war. The Fulmar was developed from the Fairey P.4/34 light bomber, which first flew on 13 January 1937, and 250 were ordered by September 1938. The first Fulmar I completed its maiden flight on 4 January 1940 at Ringway, Manchester. Although its performance was below that of land-based fighters, it was pleasant to fly and blessed with an endurance of five hours. A total of 159 were delivered in 1940, with 808 Squadron at Worthy Down, Hampshire, becoming the first frontline unit with the fighter in June 1940 and later embarking on HMS *Ark Royal*. After Fairey completed 250 Mk Is, production turned to the Mk II (including N4062, seen here) with a more powerful Rolls-Royce Merlin engine, new propeller and other changes. The last of 350 was delivered to the FAA in February 1943. Around 100 Mk IIs were converted into night fighters with AI Mk IV radar. Fulmars were withdrawn from frontline operations in February 1945.

WESTLAND WHIRLWIND

Whirlwind P7048 originally served with 137 Squadron before being transferred to Westland as a 'hack' after the fighter-bomber was withdrawn by the RAF in December 1943. On 10 October 1946, it was registered G-AGOI, but was retired before the end of 1947 and scrapped, the last extant example of its breed. Designed as an escort fighter to Specification F.37/35, the Whirlwind was the RAF's first single-seat twin-engine fighter. The first of two prototypes made its maiden flight on 11 October 1938, and a production contract was awarded in January 1939. Delivery of Whirlwind Is was delayed by problems with the airframe and the Rolls-Royce Peregrine engine – its Achilles' heel – and the first was not handed over until June 1940. After tests with 25 Squadron, in July 1940, 263 Squadron became the first unit to fully re-equip with the aircraft, undertaking its first operational sortie on 7 December 1940 from Exeter, Devon. The only other frontline operator was 137 Squadron. Only 114 Whirlwind Is (plus two prototypes) were built.

BRISTOL BEAUFIGHTER

Beaufighters served with 52 RAF squadrons as night and strike fighters. Although the prototype was built as a private venture, Specification F.17/39 was retrospectively written by the Air Ministry to authorise four prototypes and 200 production aircraft. The first flew on 17 July 1939, and the last of the four prototypes in May 1940, prior to production of Beaufighter If night fighters at the Bristol factories at Filton, Gloucestershire and Weston-super-Mare, Somerset, and by Fairey at Stockport, Manchester. Deliveries began on 12 August 1940, with the first going to the Fighter Interception Unit at Tangmere, Sussex, followed by single examples to 25, 29, 219 and 604 Squadrons in September. This radar-equipped Mk If, T4638, was with 604 'County of Middlesex' Squadron by mid-1941 and spent its entire flying career with the unit. It was involved in a 'friendly fire' incident on 2 July 1941, shooting down Wellington Ic R1516 of 311 Squadron near Mere, Wiltshire. The Beaufighter was destroyed in a fatal crash on 9 November 1941, while returning to Middle Wallop, Hampshire, after an operational sortie, which resulted in the loss of Flying Officer Michael Edmund Staples and injuries to radar operator Sergeant 'Freddie' G French.

HAWKER TYPHOON

The Typhoon became one of the most successful ground-attack aircraft of World War Two, although it was a failure in its intended role as a medium-altitude interceptor. Development was protracted because of delays to the Napier Sabre engine and the low priority given to new designs in 1940 (when the emphasis was on increasing output of existing types). Early operations were overshadowed by a series of in-flight structural failures, which required the tailplane and other sections to be strengthened. Typhoons were originally used as fighters against low-level Luftwaffe raiders from mid-1942, switching at the end of the year to ground-attack operations, initially armed with bombs, and then, from late 1943, unguided rockets. The first Typhoon unit, 56 Squadron, flew the type from 11 September 1941 to 11 May 1944, its aircraft carrying 'US' codes on their fuselages. Typhoon IB 'US-A' (EK183), depicted at Matlaske, Norfolk, on 21 April 1943, was the usual mount of Squadron Leader Thomas Henry Vincent Pheloung. New Zealander Pheloung lost his life on 20 June 1943, in EK184, which was hit by flak attacking shipping off the Hook of Holland and crashed before making it back to base. Typhoon EK183 went on to fly with 609 Squadron, surviving the war to become an instructional airframe (as 5557M) in August 1945.

HAWKER TEMPEST

Hawker conceived the Tempest as an improved version of the Typhoon – it was the Mk II version of that aircraft until March 1942. The company hoped to overcome some of the shortcomings of the Typhoon by mating a new, thinner wing with a superior finish to a strengthened fuselage with a more reliable engine. It originally planned to create variants powered by the Napier Sabre IV and II, Bristol Centaurus, and Rolls-Royce Griffon IIB and 61 engines as the Tempest I, V, II, III and IV respectively, although only the Mk II and V entered production. The first to fly was the Tempest V prototype during September 1942. The initial 100 production Mk Vs were Series I aircraft, which had the barrels for the Hispano II cannons protruding from the leading edge of the wing; the first, JN729, seen here, flew on 21 June 1943 and was retained by the manufacturer as a test bed. Around 700 Series IIs followed with 'clean' wing leading edges. Tempest Vs entered frontline service at Newchurch, Kent, during February 1944 with 3 and 486 (RNZAF) Squadrons, which were soon in action against V-1 flying-bombs over the southeast coast. A further eight squadrons re-equipped with Tempest Vs and, while most relinquished them soon after the war, 3 and 80 Squadrons continued to fly them in West Germany into early 1948.

HAWKER FURY

The first of four prototype Furies flew on 1 September 1944, one of two of the aircraft powered by the Bristol Centaurus. The third, LA610, was originally ordered as a prototype Tempest III with the Rolls-Royce Griffon IIB but emerged as a Fury powered by a Griffon 85 turning a six-blade contra-rotating propeller, with a large intake under the nose. It was rolled out in November 1944 and served as a test bed for the powerplant, although official interest in the engine waned and a Centaurus XV was installed instead, which was itself quickly replaced by a Napier Sabre VII. Low drag wing radiators allowed the nose to be redesigned with a close-fitting cowling, transforming the looks of the aircraft. The Sabre VII produced 3,500hp (2,610kW) and conferred on the Fury a maximum speed of 484mph (779km/h), making it Hawker's fastest piston-powered aircraft, with an impressive rate of climb. The fourth Fury prototype, VP207, also had a Sabre VII but, by the time it flew in 1947, official interest was focused on jet fighters. Although Hawker received an order for 100 as Fury Is for the RAF in 1944, it was cancelled in August 1946. Parallel development of a naval variant with the Centaurus led to the Sea Fury, around 860 of which were built for the FAA, Australia, Canada, Egypt, Iraq, the Netherlands and Pakistan.

WESTLAND P.14 WELKIN

In the summer of 1940, sporadic reconnaissance flights were conducted by Luftwaffe Junkers Ju 86Ps over the British Isles at altitudes above 39,000ft (11,887m), beyond the service ceiling of the defending fighters. It was clear to the Air Ministry that Germany could use a bomber at similar heights. In response, Operational Requirement OR.81 was compiled, calling for a dedicated high-altitude single-seat heavy fighter with a pressurised cabin, able to reach at least 45,000ft (13,716m) with a maximum speed above 400mph (644km/h). Both Vickers and Westland were awarded contracts to build two prototypes each, the latter as the Welkin. The first Welkin flew on 1 November 1942. The second flew in March 1943 and was extensively tested that year at the A&AEE at Boscombe Down, resulting in a production order for 100 Welkin F.Is, followed by a second for 180. Deliveries commenced in September 1943 and continued into June 1945, but as the high-altitude threat failed to materialise only 101 were delivered (26 without engines). None were used operationally, with the vast majority – including DX318 seen here – going straight into storage, where they remained until most were struck off charge in late November 1945 and scrapped.

ARMSTRONG WHITWORTH AW.38 WHITLEY

The Whitley was a monoplane twin-engined night bomber originally built to Specification B.3/34, with a crew of five. Two prototypes were built, the first flying on 17 March 1936, followed by 34 Mk Is, 46 Mk IIs and 80 Mk IIIs with different Armstrong Siddeley Tiger engine variants and armament. Rolls-Royce Merlins powered the 40 Mk IVs and IVAs. The major production version was the Whitley V, of which 1,466 were built. It had a slightly longer fuselage, modified fins with straight leading edges, rubber de-icer boots on the wings, additional fuel and provision for extra tanks in the bomb bay. The first Whitley unit in Bomber Command was 10 Squadron, which re-equipped with the aircraft in March 1937. Whitleys of 51 and 58 Squadrons made the first leaflet raid of the war on the night of 3 September 1939 over Hamburg, Bremen and the Ruhr. They also dropped the first bombs on German soil on the night of 19 March 1940, attacking the seaplane base of Hörnum on the island of Sylt, and took part in the first raid against Berlin on the night of 25–26 August. Bomber Command withdrew the Whitley from operational squadrons by May 1942, but the aircraft remained in use supporting airborne forces and as a glider-tug and with Coastal Command on anti-shipping patrols until early 1944.

VICKERS WELLINGTON

Affectionately known as the 'Wimpy' by its crews, the Vickers Wellington was built in greater numbers than any other British bomber – more than 11,460 – and also served in general reconnaissance, training and transport roles. It had a geodesic airframe that gave it great structural strength that could absorb a lot of battle damage and still remain airworthy. The prototype first flew on 15 June 1936, with the initial production aircraft appearing on 23 December 1937. Deliveries commenced in October 1938 to 99 Squadron at Mildenhall, Suffolk, the first of six Bomber Command units to re-equip with the new aircraft before the start of the war. Wellingtons from 9 and 149 Squadron made the initial raid on a German target on 4 September 1939, bombing warships at Brunsbüttel. During the night of 25–26 August 1940, Wellingtons were among other bombers striking Berlin for the first time. Wellington III X3763 served with 425 'Alouette' Squadron of the Royal Canadian Air Force from September 1942. As 'KW-E' it was hit by flak over Kiel on 13–14 October 1942, but made it back to Dishforth, Yorkshire. The aircraft (re-coded 'KW-L') and crew were lost on 15 April 1943, when it failed to return from a sortie over Stuttgart, probably falling victim to a night fighter flown by Leutnant Franze Draude of IV./NJG 4.

HANDLEY PAGE HP.52 HAMPDEN

Along with the Armstrong Whitworth Whitley and Vickers Wellington, the Hampden was one of the three medium twin-engine bombers that bore the brunt of Bomber Command operations in the early stages of the war. Designed to Specification B.9/32, the prototype Hampden made its maiden flight on 21 June 1936, followed by the production prototype the following year and the first series aircraft in May 1938. A total of 1,432 Hampdens were built, plus a further 100 as HP.53 Herefords, powered by the Napier Dagger VIII in place of the Hampden's Bristol Pegasus XVIII. Deliveries to the RAF began in September 1938, initially to 49 Squadron at Scampton, Lincolnshire, but by the start of the war 7, 44, 49, 50, 61, 76, 83, 106, 144 and 185 Squadrons also flew the bomber. Hampden I L4143, seen during a pre-delivery test flight, was one of a batch of 180 that joined the RAF between August 1938 and June 1939. It was issued to 76 Squadron and, later, went to 144 Squadron but was destroyed in a crash near Kirton in Lindsey, Lincolnshire, on the night of 22 April 1940. Flight Lieutenant Roderick Alastair Brook Learoyd of 49 Squadron became Bomber Command's first recipient of the Victoria Cross for a low-level attack in a Hampden on the Dortmund-Ems Canal on 12 August 1940. Hampdens also served as minelayers, flying 1,209 such sorties during 1940 alone. From April 1942, as it was replaced as a bomber, many were handed over to Coastal Command as Hampden TB.I torpedo-bombers. The final examples were retired from frontline units in the RAF by late 1943. Hampdens also served with the Australian, Canadian and New Zealand air forces, as well as with a single squadron of the Soviet Navy, while one was delivered to Sweden.

BRISTOL BLENHEIM IV

Although it quickly became obsolete in its original role, the Blenheim chalked up several notable achievements during World War Two: it was the only aircraft to serve with every RAF command during the conflict; it was the first RAF aircraft to cross the German frontier on 3 September 1939; it flew the initial Bomber Command raid of the conflict; and it helped pioneer night-fighting tactics using AI radar. By the start of the war, Bomber Command had already replaced its 'short nose' Blenheim Is with Mk IVs. They were heavily utilised in the escorted light-bomber missions during 1941 to entice German fighters into combat but were withdrawn from operations in Britain (but not overseas) in August 1942. This Blenheim IV, V6083, was one of 800 ordered from Rootes Securities that were delivered between October 1940 and May 1941. It served within Coastal Command with 86 Squadron and 3 School of General Reconnaissance, before transferring to 13 Operational Training Unit (as 'FV-B') and was struck off charge on 13 March 1944.

SHORT S.29 STIRLING

The Stirling was the first four-engine heavy bomber to enter service with the RAF. It was designed to Specification B.12/36, which included a clause that it should fit into a standard hangar, requiring a wingspan of less than 100ft (30.48m). This gave the bomber a high wing loading and limited its maximum altitude, shortening its frontline career. The first of two prototypes flew on 14 May 1939, preceded by the S.31 half-scale aerodynamic test bed on 19 September 1938. Deliveries to Bomber Command started with 7 Squadron at Leeming, Yorkshire, in August 1940, and Stirlings made their combat debut on the night of 10 February 1941 when three attacked oil storage tanks at Rotterdam in the Netherlands. The Stirling I was followed by the Mk III with improved Bristol Hercules engines and defensive and internal modifications. A total of 712 Stirling Is and 1,047 Mk IIIs were produced, serving with a peak of 13 Bomber Command squadrons, and they were followed by around 620 Mk IV and V transports. Stirling III BF509 was one of a batch of 200 delivered between June 1942 and May 1943. It entered service with 149 Squadron as 'DJ-B' at Lakenheath, Suffolk, later passing to 1653 Heavy Conversion Unit, established at Chedburgh in the same county in November 1943. Although the unit lost more than 50 Stirlings on operations and in accidents, BF509 survived to be struck off charge on 24 April 1945.

DE HAVILLAND DH.98 MOSQUITO

The last of 7,731 Mosquitoes built in Britain, Australia and Canada was delivered in November 1950 – ten years after the prototype made its first flight. What started as a private venture project for a fast, unarmed bomber, constructed primarily of wood, overcame significant official opposition to become one of the great aircraft of the war. The prototype made its maiden flight on 25 November 1940, its high speed and manoeuvrability helping to win over critics, leading to contracts for reconnaissance, fighter and bomber variants. Initial deliveries were photo-reconnaissance aircraft, which began flying sorties over occupied Europe on 17 September 1941. The first bomber variant was the Mosquito IV; this pair served with 627 Squadron, which specialised in marking targets for the main bomber force. The nearest aircraft, DZ353, was lost with its crew near Saint-Erblon in France on 9 June 1944 during a raid against railway targets intended to stop German reinforcements reaching Normandy, where Allied troops had fought ashore three days previously. Earlier it had flown with 105 and 139 Squadrons, the latter having the distinction of being the RAF's last frontline Mosquito bomber unit, retiring its B.35s in late 1953. The final RAF Mosquitoes were TT.35 target-tugs and T.3 conversion trainers flown until mid-1963 by 3/4 Civilian Anti-Aircraft Co-operation Unit at Exeter, Devon.

BRISTOL BEAUFORT

A total of 1,429 Bristol Beauforts were built in the UK and another 700 in Australia. They served as Coastal Command's standard torpedo-bomber from 1940 until 1943, flying with six squadrons over home waters. Four more units were based in the Mediterranean, where Beauforts based on Malta took a heavy toll on Axis shipping transporting material to North Africa. The prototype Beaufort first flew on 15 October 1938, but initial testing highlighted aspects that required detailed redesign before it was fit for service. This delayed service entry for the Beaufort I until January 1940, when 22 Squadron became the initial operator, making its first operational sorties on the night of 15–16 April laying mines. Beaufort I L9878 was delivered in the second quarter of 1940, entering service with 217 Squadron as 'MW-R' at St Eval in Cornwall, before going to 42 Squadron in late 1941. It was struck off charge at the end of May 1943. Although during 1943 the RAF replaced its Beauforts in the frontline squadrons with torpedo-carrying Bristol Beaufighters, they continued to be flown by second-line units into 1946.

FAIREY ALBACORE

Between 1939 and 1943, Fairey built 800 Albacore torpedo-bombers, which equipped 15 FAA squadrons at its peak in mid-1942. Although designed to replace the Fairey Swordfish, the Albacore only complemented the older type in service and was withdrawn before it. The prototype first flew on 12 December 1938 from Great West aerodrome (today part of London Heathrow Airport) and, after issues with cockpit heating and heavy controls were alleviated, entered production. In mid-March 1940, 826 Squadron was formed at Ford, Sussex, to become the first to fly the Albacore, going into action at the end of May against E-boats and coastal targets across the English Channel. Operations at sea began in November 1940 when 826 and 829 Squadrons embarked onboard HMS *Formidable*, attacking the Italian battleship *Vittorio Veneto* during the Battle of Cape Matapan in March 1941. Albacores also operated in the Arctic Circle in support of Russia-bound convoys, in the Western Desert, the Mediterranean, the Indian Ocean and during the invasion of North Africa. During 1943, it was replaced by the Fairey Barracuda in frontline FAA units, although 415 Squadron of the Royal Canadian Air Force still had them in June 1944 and operated over the Channel on D-Day.

FAIREY BARRACUDA

Barracuda I P9659 is seen here in the configuration adopted for dive-bombing attacks, with its Fairey-Youngman flaps extended. Although the prototype, which first flew on 7 December 1940, had its tailplane mounted on top of the fuselage, it was soon discovered that it interacted with the slipstream when the flaps were deployed in a dive, causing buffeting. The cure was a taller tail with the horizontal tailplane higher up it. The changes were tested on the second prototype, which flew on 29 June 1941. The Barracuda was designed as a torpedo- and dive-bomber to replace the Fairey Albacore and Swordfish with the FAA and, although a considerable improvement in terms of performance over the biplanes, it suffered from being overweight. The original Rolls-Royce Merlin of the Mk I (30 built) was replaced by a more powerful version of the engine in the Mk II, which became the main production variant with 1,688 built. They were followed by 852 Mk IIIs with ASV radar. The Rolls-Royce Griffon was installed in the Mk V, the final production version, which had a longer wing, enlarged fin and greater fuel capacity, but never served on aircraft carriers. Barracuda IIs entered service with 827 Squadron in January 1943 and, one year later, 12 units operated the type. The aircraft is best remembered for inflicting heavy damage on the German battleship *Tirpitz* on 3 April 1944.

SAUNDERS-ROE LERWICK AND SHRIMP

A Saunders-Roe S.36 Lerwick I at anchorage, probably at Cowes on the Isle of Wight, while the A.37 Shrimp flies overhead. Only 21 Lerwicks were produced, and they were flown by just one full RAF squadron and a Royal Canadian Air Force unit working up. Designed in response to Specification R.1/36, the Lerwick was unique as the only sleeve-valve twin-engine (powered by the Bristol Hercules) monoplane flying boat to serve in the RAF, although its service life was short and troubled. It was ordered off the drawing board in July 1937, the first flying in November 1938. Pilots quickly discovered the Lerwick was unstable, both in the air and on the water, and had a vicious stall. Although various remedies were tried, they failed to improve the flying boat's poor handling. Five Lerwick Is had been delivered by the start of the war, including three with 240 Squadron for testing, while 209 Squadron at Oban, Argyllshire, was the first to put it into operational service, making the initial patrol on Christmas Day 1939. In service, the Lerwick suffered from poor serviceability, and 209 Squadron relinquished the aircraft in May 1941, around the time the last was delivered to the RAF. The Shrimp, G-AFZS, was a half-scale test bed for the Saunders-Roe S.38 four-engine, long-range flying boat, development of which was cancelled. It first flew at Cowes in October 1939 and spent most of its time at Beaumaris on Anglesey. In 1944, it was acquired by the Ministry of Aircraft Production (becoming TK580) as a test bed for the Short Shetland and was scrapped in 1949.

SUPERMARINE SEA OTTER

The Sea Otter was the last of a long line of Supermarine biplane flying boats. It was conceived by Reginald Joseph Mitchell as a refinement of the Walrus, the most notable difference being the use of a tractor (rather than pusher) engine. Development and production of the Sea Otter was slow as Supermarine was fully occupied improving and increasing the output of Spitfires during the early years of the war. Although the first of two prototypes flew on 23 September 1938, it was not until 30 July 1943 that the first production aircraft flew in the hands of test pilot Jeffrey Quill. A contract for 190 was placed with Blackburn in 1940 but had to be cancelled when it became clear that company also did not have the spare capacity to build the amphibian. In January 1942, Saunders-Roe (Saro) on the Isle of Wight took over responsibility for production at its Columbine works at East Cowes, substituting the Bristol Perseus engine of the prototypes with the Bristol Mercury XXX. The company built 241 Sea Otter ABR.I general-purpose reconnaissance aircraft and 49 air-sea rescue ASR.IIs (including RD892 seen here) for the FAA, with around 140 Mk Is transferred to the RAF from October 1944. Additional contracts for a further 300 were cancelled soon after the end of the war.

AVRO ANSON

Anson N5331 of 6 Air Observer & Navigator School, based at Staverton, Gloucestershire, was one of 500 Mk Is delivered between October 1938 and September 1939; it was struck off charge on 16 March 1945. Ansons originally entered service in the general reconnaissance role with 48 Squadron in March 1936, becoming the first in the RAF with a retractable landing gear. A total of 13 Coastal Command squadrons flew Anson Is, and the aircraft was the first to attack a German U-boat on 5 September 1939. By the start of the war, the Anson was in the process of being replaced within Coastal Command, although it continued to fly anti-submarine patrols into 1942. The majority of Ansons built during the conflict were used as trainers. In addition to serving in training units across the British Isles, the aircraft played an important role in the Commonwealth Air Training Plan in the British Dominions (the term then used for the self-governing colonies of the Empire). Most of the 2,882 Ansons built in Canada were issued to units within the plan. The Anson X, XI and XII were communication versions of the Mk I, while the Avro XIX was adopted by the RAF as the C.19 and T.20, 21 and 22 trainers. The last of 8,138 built in Britain was a T.21 delivered in May 1952.

BLACKBURN B.26 BOTHA

The Botha was failure in its intended role of general reconnaissance, mainly because it was underpowered. Originally designed as a three-seat aircraft, the requirement was revised to add a fourth crew member and replace the Bristol Perseus engine with the more powerful Bristol Taurus, but, as these were in short supply, the Botha reverted to using the Perseus. The first of two prototypes made its maiden flight on 28 December 1938, by when the aircraft had already been ordered, resulting in production lines being established at Brough, Yorkshire, and Dumbarton, West Dunbartonshire. In July 1939, the first production Botha I appeared and was used for trials at the Torpedo Development Unit at Gosport, Hampshire, prior to deliveries to the RAF beginning in earnest. From October 1939, 608 Squadron replaced its Avro Ansons with Botha Is, flying anti-submarine patrols from Thornaby, Yorkshire, but it was destined to be the only frontline unit with the type, withdrawing them in November 1940. Many of the 580 Bothas built were employed as trainers at various Bombing and Gunnery Schools (B&GSs), Radio Schools and at 3 School of General Reconnaissance, while a few were equipped with target-towing gear. The final Bothas were withdrawn in September 1944.

FAIREY BATTLE

As a light bomber, the Fairey Battle proved woefully inadequate, suffering high losses during the Battle of France in 1940. Quickly replaced in the front line, Battles were issued to units of the British Commonwealth Air Training Plan in Australia, Canada, South Africa and Southern Rhodesia (now Zimbabwe). Battle I L5480 was delivered to 24 Maintenance Unit at Ternhill, Shropshire, in January 1940. The following month, it was allocated to the Royal Canadian Air Force as 1639, shipped across the Atlantic and taken on charge at Trenton, Ontario, on 29 April 1940. The aircraft was briefly flown by the Test & Development Flight before being issued in June 1940 to 1 Training Command at Toronto, Ontario, for use at one of its four B&GSs. The open rear position was not suited to gunnery training in the Canadian climate; 1639 was one of 212 Battles fitted with a Bristol manually operated turret, the modification occurring in mid-1942, after which it served with 9 B&GS at Mont Joli, Quebec, within 3 Training Command. It survived the war to be sold for scrap in June 1946.

BOULTON PAUL P.82 DEFIANT

While the Defiant is most often remembered as a night fighter, serving with 13 RAF squadrons at its peak, the aircraft was originally designed as a day fighter. Stripped of the powered turret and fitted with a target sleeve and wind-driven winch, the aircraft played an important, if unsung, role towing targets. Defiant TT.I (Trop) AA591 was built as a Mk II and taken on charge in February 1942 at 24 Maintenance Unit (MU) at Ternhill, Shropshire, transferring to 9 MU at Cosford in the same county that April. In September 1943, it was converted into a TT.I target-tug, but remained in store with 10 MU at Hullavington, Wiltshire, until going to 47 MU, a packing and storage depot at Sealand in Wales, before being shipped to Karachi, then in India, between January and March 1944. It was issued to 22 Anti-Aircraft Co-operation Unit, which operated all over India, and is seen at Tezgaon, outside Dhaka, on 14 June 1944. The Defiant was struck off charge on 21 June 1945.

VICKERS WARWICK

Vickers designed the Warwick as a heavier version of its Wellington bomber, but development was protracted because of difficulty finding a suitable engine. The prototype first flew on 13 August 1939 powered by the unreliable Rolls-Royce Vulture, and the second prototype used the Bristol Centaurus, but by the time the first Mk I flew on 1 May 1942, it had Pratt & Whitney Double Wasps. It was rejected as a bomber after only 16 B.Is were built and was adopted for long-range air-sea rescue as the ASR.I. Fourteen were modified as Warwick C.Is for use by BOAC on the mail service to North Africa and the Mediterranean from February 1943. This aircraft, originally BV256, was the last modified, becoming G-AGFK. BOAC returned the Warwick to the RAF as BV256 in early 1944, and it joined 525 Squadron when it formed at Weston Zoyland in Somerset on 2 September that year. The unit initially flew passengers to Gibraltar but had extended services to various points in North Africa by March 1944. After suffering two accidents in May, the Warwick C.Is were relegated to carrying freight only until replaced by Douglas Dakotas in June 1944. Most of the unit's Warwick C.Is passed to 167 Squadron, but not BV256. It was officially struck off charge in July 1947.

AVRO 685 YORK

The York was one of the few transport aircraft developed in Britain during World War Two. It used much of the Lancaster airframe, mated to a new fuselage, to create a long-range transport to Specification C.1/42. The first of four prototypes, LV626, seen here, made its maiden flight on 5 July 1942, but development proceeded slowly, as production of combat aircraft had priority. The third York prototype was the first to enter service, going to 24 Squadron as *Ascalon* in May 1943, equipped as a VIP transport. It was used to ferry high-ranking personnel – including Prime Minister Winston Churchill and King George VI – to various conferences and on inspection tours. RAF York Is were configured with passenger, freight or combined passenger/freight interiors, with 511 Squadron at Lyneham, Wiltshire, becoming the first to receive the aircraft for 'traditional' transport duties during November 1943, but only became fully equipped with the aircraft in early 1945. The last of the 208 built for the RAF was delivered in April 1948. Yorks accounted for nearly half of the total tonnage airlifted into Berlin by the RAF during the Soviet blockade of the German city in 1948–49.

AUSTER

The Battle of France highlighted the limited utility and vulnerability of the Westland Lysander army co-operation aircraft in combat zones. It prompted the British military to investigation the role lighter aircraft could play supporting troops in the field, spotting for the artillery and providing communications between formations. These experiments resulted in large orders being placed with British Taylorcraft of Rearsby, Leicestershire, for the Auster, a military variant developed from the Plus C. The Plus C was itself the British equivalent of the US Taylorcraft Aviation Company Model A. More than 1,600 Austers of four variants were produced during the war. Auster III NJ747, see here, was the first of a batch of 224 of the variant delivered between June and September 1943. It served only with 654 Squadron in North Africa and Italy and was struck off charge on 29 November 1945. After the war, many Austers were sold to private owners, and the company went on to develop a range of aircraft specifically for the civil market.

DE HAVILLAND DH.82 TIGER MOTH

A generation of British pilots learnt the basics of flight on the Tiger Moth. Tiger Moth II R5130 was one of a batch of 400 delivered between December 1939 and May 1940, some going to the air forces of Australia, New Zealand, South Africa and Southern Rhodesia (Zimbabwe). This aircraft was delivered on 5 April 1940, entered service with 3 Ferry Pilots Pool and was last used by 63 Group Communications Flight at Hawarden outside Cheshire. It was sold in November 1953 to Rollason of Croydon, London, registered as G-APOV in August 1958 and converted by the company in 1960 as a Thruxton Jackaroo, a four-seat cabin modification of the Tiger Moth. Its flying career as a Jackaroo was brief, however, as it was damaged beyond repair on 3 July 1961, after crashing at Hawkenbury Farm in Staplehurst, Kent. By 1964, its remains were with the Staplefield Place School at Handcross in Sussex, where it lasted until 5 November 1969, when it went up in flames in lieu of Guy Fawkes.

MILES MAGISTER AND MASTER, AND AIRSPEED OXFORD

The Empire Central Flying School (ECFS) was formed at Hullavington, Wiltshire, on 1 April 1942, to teach and maintain standards of instruction techniques in various aircraft, with most of its personnel coming from the Central Flying School (CFS). Among the types on strength was (front to rear) the Miles Magister I elementary trainer, Miles Master III advanced trainer and Airspeed Oxford I multi-engine trainer. The prototype Magister first flew on 20 March 1937. Magister N3838 was one of a batch of 204 delivered between October 1938 and February 1939, initially joining 15 Elementary Flying Training School. It survived the war to be sold on 18 March 1946. Just over 1,300 Magisters were built, many joining the civil register after the war as Hawk Trainer IIIs. Master III W8962 spent its entire flying career with the ECFS, being struck off charge on 14 May 1944. A total of 3,249 Masters were built. The majority were used as trainers, but some served as glider-tugs or target-tugs, while a dedicated derivative for the latter role was produced as the Martinet. Oxford I DF233 was delivered in 1942, serving with the CFS and 9 Pilots Advanced Flying Unit before joining the ECFS. It was struck off charge on 22 June 1950.

GENERAL AVIATION GAL48 HOTSPUR

The success of German glider-borne troops capturing the Belgian fort at Eben Emael on 10 May 1940 resulted in a desperate drive to create similar airborne forces within the British military. As part of this process Specification 10/40 was written, outlining an assault glider similar to the German DFS 230. General Aviation responded with the Hotspur. While the Hotspur could carry eight troops, including the pilot, it failed to reach the desired gliding range of 100 miles (161km) with a full load from 20,000ft (6,096m), resulting in its relegation to the training role after only 22 of the Hotspur I operational variant were produced. They were followed by over 1,000 Mk II and IIIs, which were used to train soldiers of the Army's Glider Pilot Regiment to fly and provide fight experience to troops destined to ride into battle in larger operational types. Most Hotspurs were flown by the five Glider Training Schools (GTSs), including this pair of Mk IIs of 2 GTS based at Weston-on-the-Green in Oxfordshire in 1942.

ARMSTRONG WHITWORTH AW.52G

Armstrong Whitworth's chief designer, John 'Jimmy' Lloyd, became interested in laminar flow and boundary layer control in conjunction with all-wing airframes early in World War Two. Laminar flow aerofoils have low aerodynamic friction with a smooth flow of air over their surfaces. Boundary layer control seeks to maintain the smooth flow over the wing for as long as possible. The project used the in-house designation AW.52 and by September 1943 had progressed to the testing of models in wind tunnels at Whitley, outside Coventry, Warwickshire. To test the low-speed characteristics of a proposed jet-powered flying wing, the building of a two-seat glider was authorised – the AW.52G – with laminar flow and boundary layer control using suction pumps. Armstrong Whitworth began construction of the wooden AW.52G (RG324) at Whitley in 1944, moving to nearby Baginton for completion early in the following year. The project had a low priority, as the company was busy with wartime production programmes, so it was not until 2 March 1945 that it was towed aloft and released for the first time from an Armstrong Whitworth Whitley V. Most of the early flights were undertaken by Charles Turner-Hughes. From 20,000ft (6,096m), the AW.52G glided for around 25mins before landing.

GLOSTER E.28/39

In August 1939, the Air Ministry agreed to build a jet-powered aircraft using an engine designed by Flight Lieutenant Frank Whittle and built by Power Jets. Gloster's chief designer, (Wilfred) George Carter, knew Whittle and on 3 February 1940, the friendship proved useful when his company was awarded a contract to build two aircraft to Specification E.28/39, which outlined a test bed for the power plant that could be developed as an interceptor. The pair collaborated closely on the project. Initial construction work on both E.28/39s was undertaken at Hucclecote, Gloucestershire, but the first, W4041, was later dispersed to the premises of Regent Motors in nearby Cheltenham to remove the possibility of both being destroyed in a single German bombing raid. It returned to Hucclecote on 7 April 1941, fitted with a W.1X engine for taxi trials. The following day, test pilot Phillip Edward Gerald Sayer 'hopped' the E.28/39 6ft (1.83m) off the ground three times during a taxi run. Cranwell in Lincolnshire was selected for flight tests because of its long runway and location away from population centres. The prototype was transported there by road and fitted with a flightworthy W.1. At 1945hrs on 15 May, Sayer lined up on the runway, opened up the W.1 to its maximum 16,500 revolutions to produce 860lb (3.8kN) of thrust and, after a take-off run of 1,500 to 1,800ft (457 to 549m), lifted off from the runway. After 17mins airborne, Sayer landed safely back at Cranwell, having opened a new chapter for British aviation.

CHAPTER 8

POST-WAR
RISE OF THE JET

While developments and improvements continued during the relative peace of the early post-war years, there was one landmark development that would define the next phase in aviation: the transition from piston to jet engines.

By the end of World War Two, piston-engined fighters were approaching the peak of their potential in terms of performance, while the first generation of jet aircraft had begun to enter service with the RAF. The signing of the official surrender documents by Japan on the battleship USS *Missouri* in Tokyo Bay on 2 September 1945 allowed a rationalisation of ongoing aircraft development programmes. A plethora of new and improved variants of existing aircraft, once expected to play a role in the conflict, was no longer needed. Although many projects were cancelled outright, others were allowed to continue, at least to the prototype stage. Unlike after the Great War, when the RAF had to 'make do' with its existing stock of aircraft, the official policy was to continue to introduce new types into service, although in far smaller quantities than during the war, with piston-engined aircraft slowing giving way to the jets. While this permitted the aviation industry to continue to design and develop new military aircraft, it could not support the large number of major manufacturers and numerous subcontractors active throughout the conflict. No official plan to rationalise the industry was implemented in the immediate post-war years, but, by 1950, several famous companies had ceased business.

AVRO LANCASTER

Three Avro Lancaster B.I(FE)s of 35 Squadron, based at Graveley, Huntingdon, are seen here just prior to leaving for a goodwill tour of the United States, known as Operation *Lancaster*. The squadron departed in two flights, each with eight Lancasters, across the Atlantic for Mitchel Field in New York on 8 and 9 July 1946, staging via St Mawgan in Cornwall, Lagens in the Azores and Gander, Newfoundland, in Canada. They arrived at Mitchel Field on 16 July and, two days later, the squadron flew a formation of 12 aircraft over New York City. Other stops on the tour, before returning to Mitchel, were: Scott Field in St Louis, Illinois; Lowry Field in Denver, Colorado; Long Beach, California; Kelly Field in San Antonio, Texas; Andrews Field, Washington DC; and Westover, Boston, Massachusetts. Twelve Lancasters participated in the American Air Forces Day Flying Display on 1 August, flying in formation over several Californian cities and towns. Soon after returning to Graveley on 29 August, the squadron moved to Stradishall in Suffolk.

AVRO 694 LINCOLN

The Lincoln was conceived as a further development of the Avro Lancaster for operations against Japan. The first of three prototypes made its maiden flight on 9 June 1944 from Ringway, Manchester, and a total of 82 Lincoln B.Is and 447 B.IIs were built. Lincolns were assembled by Armstrong Whitworth and Metropolitan-Vickers, in addition to Avro. During August 1945, 57 Squadron based at RAF East Kirkby, Lincolnshire, became the first frontline unit with the new heavy bomber. This aircraft, Lincoln B.II RF385, was built by Armstrong Whitworth and issued to 57 Squadron. Its career was brief, as it crashed near Barsby, Leicestershire, on 20 February 1946, after control was lost while flying in clouds. Bomber Command had 20 Lincoln-equipped squadrons at its peak in 1950, by when the aircraft was already considered obsolete. Lincolns flew operational sorties in RAF service during the Malayan Emergency and against the Mau Mau uprising in Kenya. They were also flown by 90 Group (Signals Command) for calibration and as electronic countermeasures trainers, and it was 151 Squadron (the former Signals Command Development Squadron) that operated the RAF's final examples into 1963. Lincolns were also produced in Australia and Canada for their air forces, and also served in Argentina.

SHORT STURGEON

Only 28 Sturgeons were built, comprising four prototypes (two S.1s and two TT.2s), 23 production TT.2 target-tugs and a single SB.3 (a second was a converted airframe). Three prototypes were ordered in October 1943 as carrier-borne reconnaissance and bomber aircraft for service with the FAA in the Pacific. It was the first twin-engine carrier-based aircraft specifically designed for the Royal Navy, but the programme progressed slowly. This is the first prototype Sturgeon S.1, RK787, which flew from Rochester in Kent, on 7 June 1946, with Geoffrey Tyson at the controls. It was displayed at Farnborough, Hampshire, in late June, and at the Society of British Aircraft Constructors show at Radlett in early September 1946. On 25 April 1947, it went back to Farnborough for arrestor gear trials, passing to the A&AEE at Boscombe Down, Wiltshire, on 8 May, with which the aircraft was used for deck landing trials on the aircraft carrier HMS *Illustrious*. A second series of tests on the same carrier ended prematurely on 8 October when the arrestor hook failed. By April 1948, the wreck was at Rochester, acting as a source of spares for the second prototype.

DE HAVILLAND DH.103 HORNET

The Hornet was one of the most beautiful piston-engined fighters ever built. It was designed as a private venture single-seat, twin-engine strike fighter, around which the Air Ministry wrote Specification F.12/43 and ordered two prototypes. The first made its maiden flight on 28 July 1944 and quickly proved to be faster than the early Gloster Meteor jets. Hornet F.1s were ordered for use in the Pacific campaign, but the end of hostilities curtailed production after only 60 were built. A small number of photo-reconnaissance Hornet PR.2s followed, but the main production variant was the F.3, which had an extended dorsal fin fillet, greater fuel capacity and provision to carry bombs or rocket projectiles under the wings. The last variant for the RAF was the Hornet F.4 with a camera in the fuselage, but it only accounted for 12 of the 200 of all versions built for the RAF. Hornets had the distinction of being the last piston-engined fighter in RAF squadron service. They served with 19, 41 (to which these four belonged), 64 and 65 Squadrons of Fighter Command between early 1946 and early 1951, and with 33, 45 and 80 Squadrons in the Far East from April 1951, 45 Squadron retiring the last Hornets in June 1955.

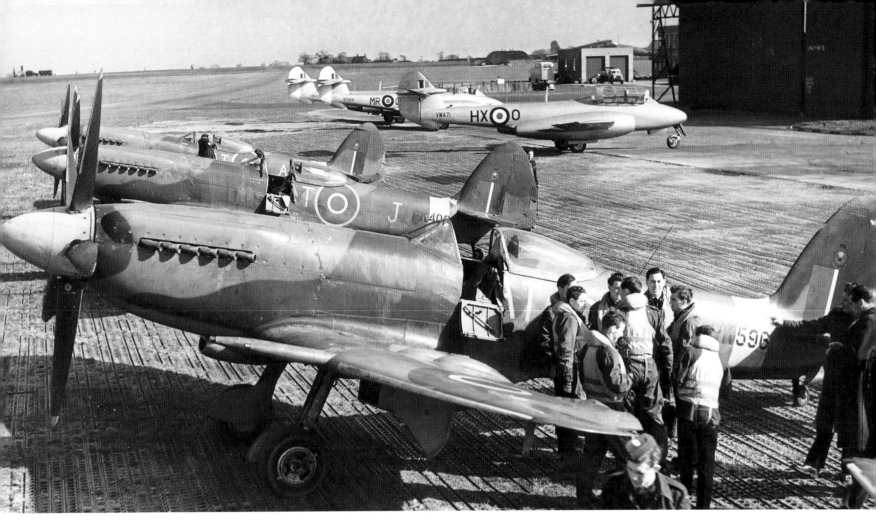

SUPERMARINE SPITFIRE

Three Spitfire F.22s of 613 'City of Manchester' Squadron of the Royal Auxiliary Air Force on pierced steel planking at Horsham St Faith, Norfolk, in March 1950. Based at Ringway, Manchester, the squadron flew the Rolls-Royce Griffon-powered F.22 between July 1948 and March 1951, frequently deploying to other airfields for exercises and 'summer camps'. In April 1950, the squadron's code prefix changed from 'RAT' to 'Q3', marking its transfer from Reserve to Fighter Command. The nearest aircraft, PK596, was delivered to 33 Maintenance Unit at Lyneham, Wiltshire, in November 1945 and issued to 613 Squadron on 10 November 1948, as 'RAT-L'. It passed to 103 Flying Refresher School at Full Sutton, in the East Riding of Yorkshire, on 16 June 1951, was declared as 'non-effective stock' exactly two years later and sold for scrap in May 1954. In the distance are three Gloster Meteors, including T.7 VW471 'HX-O' of 203 Advanced Flying School from Stradishall, Suffolk, and a pair of F.4s of 245 Squadron (including VT109 'MR-O') based at Horsham St Faith.

SUPERMARINE SEAFANG

The ultimate piston-engined development of the Spitfire was the Seafang, designed to operate from the Royal Navy's aircraft carriers. It was created as a naval equivalent of the Spiteful fighter, with the same laminar-flow wing but with an arrestor hook for deck landings. A contract for 150 interim Seafang F.31s was placed in May 1945 to provide a pool of aircraft while the definitive F.32 was developed. The Seafang F.32 had a contra-rotating propeller to eliminate the 'swing' caused by the torque of the Rolls-Royce Griffin engine while alighting on a carrier, plus folding wings. The first Seafang to fly was F.31 VG471, seen here, which was delivered to Farnborough on 15 January 1946. The F.32 prototype, VB895, flew in early 1946, going to Farnborough in June 1946 for deck arrestor tests. Test pilot Lieutenant Commander Mike Lithgow in VB895 performed eight landings on the aircraft carrier HMS *Illustrious* on 21 May 1947, but, by then, Admiralty interest in the Seafang had lapsed. The aircraft was also demonstrated to American, Dutch and French officials in August 1946, but no orders were forthcoming. Only ten Seafangs were completed (and several others delivered dismantled), and little use was made of the aircraft.

FAIREY FIREFLY

Post-war, the armed forces of Europe were re-established with equipment supplied by the victorious powers. The Firefly was adopted by the Royal Netherlands Navy, receiving 20 F.Is and ten FR.Is in the first half of 1946, which entered service with 860, 861 and 1 Squadrons. The first delivered was originally built for the Royal Navy as PP458, becoming '6-1' in Dutch service. Between June 1947 and February 1948, it was converted by Fairey as a T.1 two-seat conversion trainer, after which it re-entered service with the Royal Netherlands Navy as '12-11'. Two other Mk Is were also modified as two-seaters by Aviolanda at Papendrecht, using parts supplied by Fairey. The Dutch company also modified four aircraft as T.2 operational trainers, two each in both 1949 and 1951. In 1947, the fleet was augmented by 40 new Firefly FR.4s, followed by 14 NF.5s in 1949 and a final batch of four former Royal Canadian Navy AS.5s in February 1953. Firefly T.1 '12-11' crashed on 22 September 1959 and was subsequently scrapped. The last Dutch Fireflies were retired in 1961.

BLACKBURN FIREBRAND

Although conceived in 1940 and first flown in February 1942, the Blackburn Firebrand suffered a protracted development and saw no service during the war. Three prototypes and nine production Firebrand F.I fighters were produced, before work turned to the TF.II torpedo strike fighter, only 12 of which were built. The radial Bristol Centaurus IX replaced the inline Napier Sabre from the TF.III, but most of the 25 produced were later modified as TF.IVs with a larger fin and rudder. Firebrand EK726 was one of 103 TF.IVs built between May 1945 and January 1946, of which 63 were later converted into TF.Vs with horn-balanced elevators and longer span aileron tabs. Production of the TF.V (and VA) ended in late 1947, after 150 aircraft had been built. The first operational Firebrand unit was 813 Squadron with TF.IVs, formed on 1 September 1945, although it disbanded on 30 September 1946, having never served on a carrier. The unit was revived with TF.Vs on 1 May 1947, taking them onto HMS *Illustrious* in September 1947, and then onto HMS *Implacable* for nine weeks during 1948 and six months in 1949, before moving to HMS *Indomitable*. It re-equipped with Westland Wyverns in August 1953. The only other frontline unit with Firebrands was 827 Squadron, which operated TF.5s (as the TF.V became in June 1948) from December 1950 to December 1952, with cruises on HMS *Illustrious* and *Eagle*.

BLACKBURN B.48 FIRECREST

Blackburn's desire to create an improved Firebrand naval strike fighter was hampered by prolonged development and changing technical requirements and ultimately resulted in an aircraft deemed unsuitable to operate from an aircraft carrier. Known within the company as the Firecrest, the Blackburn B.48 was officially the S.28/43 after the specification that spawned it. Initially conceived as a Firebrand with a laminar flow wing with an inverted gull profile, the fuselage required redesign to accommodate the specified Bristol Centaurus 77 with a contra-rotating propeller, which permitted a smaller rudder than that of the Firebrand. The cockpit was moved forward to improve the pilot's view. Two prototypes were ordered on 1 January 1944, and a third added later, but a proposal for an additional three powered by the Napier E.122 diverted resources and slowed development until it was dropped in October 1945. In January 1946, Bristol ended work on the Centaurus 77, and the single propeller Centaurus 59 was substituted, at the penalty of requiring a larger rudder. Prior to the prototype, RT651, making its first flight on 1 April 1947, the Ministry of Supply determined that the Firecrest would need strengthening if it were to serve as a strike fighter and thus declined to place a production contract. The second, RT656, was used for structural tests and not flown, while the third, VF172, tested power-boosted ailerons. Flight testing ended in March 1949.

GLOSTER METEOR

The RAF High Speed Flight was reformed on 14 June 1946, at Tangmere, West Sussex, with the aim of breaking the world air speed record with the Gloster Meteor. Flying Meteor F.IV EE454, Group Captain Hugh Joseph Wilson raised the record to 606.26mph (975.68km/h) on 7 November 1945. In August 1946, Meteor F.IV EE549, seen here, was delivered to the Flight direct from the Gloster Aircraft Company, with uprated Rolls-Royce Derwents, all armament removed (and gun ports covered) and a modified canopy with small portholes. Group Captain Edward 'Teddy' Mortlock Donaldson flew EE549 on 7 September to set a new record of 615.78mph (990.79km/h) off the coast at Rustington, Sussex. With its job done, the Flight disbanded on 30 September 1946, although, in January 1947, after display at the Paris Air Show, EE549 set a new record time of 20mins 11secs between Le Bourget and Croydon in London. The aircraft later served with the Fighter Command Communications Squadron and Central Fighter Establishment, before becoming an instructional airframe at Cranwell, Lincolnshire, in June 1952. In early 2021, it was displayed at the Tangmere Military Aviation Museum, on the site of the former RAF airfield.

DE HAVILLAND DH.100 VAMPIRE

Five Vampire F.1s of 501 Squadron of the Royal Auxiliary Air Force flying over Bristol in February 1950. The unit flew the aircraft between November 1948 and June 1951 from Filton, Gloucestershire. The Vampire was the second jet aircraft to enter service with the RAF and was originally known as the Spider Crab, the prototype first flying on 24 August 1943, while Geoffrey de Havilland, Junior was undertaking high-speed taxi runs, although the first official flight took place on 20 September. Two further prototypes were completed and flown before the end of the war, as was the first production Vampire F.1, which made its maiden flight on 20 April 1945. Vampires did not enter frontline service until April 1946, however, when 247 Squadron re-equipped at Chilbolton, Hampshire, the first of 11 squadrons, including five auxiliary units, that flew the initial variant. Production of Vampire F.1s for the RAF was sub-contracted to English Electric, while 70 were also built for Sweden.

ARMSTRONG WHITWORTH AW.52

Armstrong Whitworth built two AW.52s as sub-scale test beds for proposed large flying-wing airliner and bomber concepts. The company put forward a design study in March 1944 for an experimental, tailless twin jet aircraft with a similar configuration to the AW.52G glider test bed. Specification E.9/44 was written around the aircraft and Armstrong Whitworth received a contract on 25 August 1944 to build two. Although Metropolitan-Vickers F2 Mk 4 engines were originally specified, the company was instructed to install Rolls-Royce RB.41 Nene 2s in the first AW.52, TS363, which made its maiden flight from Boscombe Down in the hands of Eric Franklin on 13 November 1947. The second AW.52, TS368, had less powerful Rolls-Royce RB.37 Derwent 5s, flying on 1 September 1948. On 30 May 1949, test pilot John Lancaster in TS368 experienced a violent pitching oscillation and was forced to eject, becoming the first person to successfully escape from a British aircraft using an ejector seat. The surviving aircraft was transferred to Farnborough in October 1950, for research into laminar flow and airflow behaviour. It was dismantled in May 1954.

SUPERMARINE ATTACKER

Specification E.1/45 covered the production of two Supermarine Type 398 prototypes of the Attacker naval fighter, the first of which (TS413, seen here) made its maiden flight on 17 June 1947, flown by test pilot Mike Lithgow. The Attacker had the laminar-flow wing of the Seafang mated to a new fuselage incorporating a Rolls-Royce Nene 3. The Type 398s were preceded by a single Type 392 (TS409), which Jeffrey Quill piloted for its first flight on 27 July 1946. The Type 398 differed from the 392 by having a Martin-Baker ejector seat, yoke-style arrestor hook, long-stroke landing gear, catapult strop attachment points, provision for rocket-assisted take-off gear and spoilers. The third airframe (second Type 398) had larger engine inlets and the wing moved aft by 13.5in (34cm). On 27 February 1948, Lithgow flew an Attacker around a 62-mile (100km) closed circuit to set a speed record of 565mph (909km/h). Production as the Attacker F.1 was authorised in September 1948, and the aircraft entered FAA service in August 1951, flying with frontline and reserve squadrons for six years. A total of 182 Attackers were built, including the prototypes and F.1 (43), FB.1 (16) and FB.2 (84) production versions, plus 36 de-navalised aircraft for the Royal Pakistan Air Force.

HAWKER P.1040

In February 1946, Hawker was authorised to produce three P.1040 prototypes and a structural test airframe after the design raised the interest of the Naval Staff. The first was VP401, an aerodynamic research aircraft, built at Hawker's factory at Langley, Berkshire, but transported to Boscombe Down for its first flight to take advantage of the long, hard runway there. During the jet's maiden flight on 2 September 1947, test pilot William Humble noted severe vibration in the airframe. Three days later, VP401 went to Farnborough for tests with the RAE, where the problem was corrected by redesigning the heat shields that protected the fuselage sides from the jet efflux. Early in 1949, the original Rolls-Royce Nene 1 was replaced by a more powerful Nene 101 prior to entry in the National Air Races at Elmdon, Birmingham. On 30 July 1949, Squadron Leader Neville Duke won the Kemsley Challenge Trophy at the race and, two days later, Squadron Leader Trevor Sidney 'Wimpy' Wade won the SBAC Trophy, while both pilots shared the Geoffrey de Havilland Memorial Trophy for the fastest lap, at an average of 563mph (906km/h). In November 1949, Hawker received a contract for a production version of the P.1040, by then known as the Sea Hawk. The following year, VP401 had an Armstrong Siddeley Snarler rocket motor installed in the rear fuselage, becoming the sole P.1072.

PERCIVAL PRENTICE

The Prentice was designed as an elementary trainer to replace the de Havilland Tiger Moth, with accommodation for two pupils and an instructor. The first of four prototypes made its maiden flight on 31 March 1946, while most of the 19 pre-production aircraft delivered from November 1947 were used to undertake a full-scale evaluation within the training syllabus. One of these, VN684, was employed to investigate the trainer's potentially dangerous spin characteristics. The tests were required after it was discovered the Prentice could enter a flat spin, which was difficult to recover from. Prentice VN684 was fitted with a small parachute to ease exit from the spin, which was contained within a box strapped on the top of the rear fuselage, and a guard at the top of the fin to stop it fowling the rudder. Trials resulted in production aircraft having the tailplane moved forward and a larger fin and rudder, as well as fuselage strakes and upturned wing tips. Around 370 production aircraft were ordered for the RAF, with exports to Argentina and licence production in India. Aviation Traders bought 252 former RAF Prentices in 1956 for sale on the civil market, but fewer than 30 eventually passed into private ownership.

VICKERS VALETTA

The Valetta was a military derivative of the Viking commercial transport procured to replace the Douglas Dakotas flown by the RAF tactical transport squadrons. The prototype made its maiden flight on 30 June 1947, and 209 Valetta C.1s were delivered between March 1948 and January 1952. Valettas first entered service in May 1949 with 204 Squadron at Kabrit in Egypt. The aircraft was issued to another six squadrons in the Middle East and Aden (Yemen), three in the Far East and four in the British Isles, including 622 Squadron, the only transport unit of the Royal Auxiliary Air Force. The RAF also received 12 Valetta C.2 VIP transports and 40 T.3 navigator trainers, while 18 T.3s were later converted into T.4 radar trainers. Valetta C.2 prototype VL262 first flew on 22 January 1948, and, by March, was assigned to the Airborne Forces Experimental Establishment at Beaulieu, Hampshire, for glider-towing trials. It is understood to be the aircraft depicted here towing an Airspeed Horsa glider. Little use was made of assault gliders after the war and Valettas were not called upon to serve as tugs in squadron service. The last Valetta flown by the RAF, a C.2 assigned to the Commander-in-Chief of RAF Germany, was retired in June 1969.

HANDLEY PAGE HASTINGS

A four-engine military heavy transport, the Hastings was designed to Specification C.3/44 as a replacement for the Avro York. It was the backbone of RAF Transport Command's airlift capability from the late-1940s to the early-1960s. The prototype Hastings, TE580, seen here, made its maiden flight from Wittering, Northamptonshire, on 7 May 1946, with Squadron Leader Maurice Hartford at the controls, with the second aircraft flying on 25 April 1947. RAF transport versions were the Hastings C.1; the C.2 with increased fuel, a wider tailplane and more powerful Bristol Hercules engines; and the C.1A (an upgraded C.1 with many features of the C.2); plus the VIP configured C.4, four of which were delivered. The first RAF unit with the new transport was 47 Squadron in September 1948, which along with 267 Squadron was soon involved in the airlift to lift the blockade around the besieged city of Berlin. Seven additional squadrons flew Hastings transports in Britain, while others operated the type overseas. A total of 151 Hastings (plus two prototypes) were built by 1952, with all except four C.3s delivered to New Zealand going to the RAF.

CHAPTER 9

THE POST-WAR YEARS
A NEW GENERATION OF AIRLINERS

It was hoped the lifting of wartime restrictions on private and commercial flying would fuel demand for new civil aircraft. The British industry hoped to cash in with a new generation of designs. Development of commercial airliners all but ceased in Britain during the years of World War Two, although planning for civil aviation requirements began in 1942. The Brabazon Committee, named after its chair, Lord Brabazon of Tara, was tasked with making recommendations for the post-war civil aviation requirements of the British Empire and Commonwealth, meeting between December 1942 and February 1943. A second committee, under the same chair, was appointed on 25 May 1943 to expand upon the work of the first. It issued various papers between August 1943 and December 1945 outlining requirements for several different classes of airliners, development of which was contracted out to the industry towards the end of the war. It was hoped that the advances in performance and passenger comfort of the new designs would persuade airlines across the globe to replace the interim types – little more than modified bombers or flying boats in most cases – adopted when hostilities ended. The problem the aviation industry faced was the large numbers of surplus military transports available for a fraction of the price of a new aircraft.

AVRO 691 LANCASTRIAN

The Lancastrian was a stopgap transport conversion of the Lancaster bomber produced for both the RAF – C.II and IV – and as a commercial airliner – I and III. The Mk I and II could accommodate nine passengers, with up to 13 in the Mk III and IV. The prototype, G-AGLF flew on 17 January 1945 and 21 Mk Is were delivered to BOAC. Silver City Airways Lancastrian IIIs *City of Canberra* and *City of London* were originally part of British South American Airways' order for 18 Mk IIIs, only six of which were delivered before the company was absorbed by BOAC. The other 12 were sold to other companies, with British Aviation Services acquiring three for use by Silver City in October 1946, its initial aircraft.

SHORT S.25 SANDRINGHAM

By installing an airliner interior into the Sunderland maritime reconnaissance and anti-submarine aircraft, Short was quickly able to create the Sandringham for use on long-range commercial flying boat services. Sunderland III ML788 was built at the Short facility on the river Medway at Rochester, Kent. It was delivered to BOAC on 28 July 1944, as G-AGKX, one of 24 Sunderlands operated by the airline. From late 1943, they flew from Poole Harbour in Dorset to Cairo and on to Karachi, the service being extended to Calcutta in May 1944. As this route passed through military controlled areas, the aircraft carried Transport Command codes ('OQZF' on G-AGKX) and many also retained their former RAF identities. Post-war, most of BOAC's Sunderlands were refurbished with more suitable interiors as the airline's Hythe class. For G-AGKX (as ML788), the process went beyond making passengers more comfortable, as the nose and tail cone were faired over to create the first (and only) Sandringham 1. Inside, the aircraft was configured for 24 day or 16 'sleeper' passengers. It was relaunched onto the Medway after modification in late November 1945, received a Certificate of Airworthiness in January 1946 and was redelivered (again as G-AGKX) to BOAC that June with the name *Himalaya*. In May 1949, British charter and schedule operator Aquila Airways bought *Himalaya*, operating the flying boat until it was withdrawn in early 1953. A further 26 Sandringhams (of six different variants) were produced by Short at Belfast, Northern Ireland, from existing Sunderland airframes.

BRISTOL 170

The first new British civil airliner to fly after the war was the Bristol 170. Conceived as a rugged transport for service in the Far East, it was built as the Wayfarer airliner and as the Freighter, with large nose doors for cargo. The prototype, G-AGPV, was completed as a Freighter, serving as an aerodynamic test bed for the aircraft. It made its maiden flight at Filton, Gloucestershire, on 2 December 1945, with test pilot Cyril Frank Uwins at the controls. The aircraft was handed over to the Air Ministry as VR380 on 28 September 1946 for evaluation at the A&AEE at Boscombe Down. The following month, it returned to Filton and was converted into a Wayfarer, with new wing tips increasing span by 4ft (1.2m) and the addition of square passenger windows. Between 1948 and 1956, it served as a radar test bed with the Telecommunications Research Establishment at Defford, Worcestershire, in support of the Gloster Javelin fighter programme. It was sold in August 1956, going on to fly with a number of civil operators, and was finally scrapped in 1965. Bristol built a total of 214 Freighters, including 16 Wayfarers.

AVRO TUDOR

The Avro 688 Tudor I was the first British transport with a pressurised cabin. It was designed to Specification 29/43, issued to Avro in March 1944, and two prototypes were ordered that September. The first flew on 14 June 1945, but displayed directional and longitudinal instability, pre-stall wing buffeting and bounced landing at heavy weights, problems that required a significant amount of work to alleviate. Although BOAC had ordered 20, in April 1947 it rejected the Tudor I as incapable of operating on its Atlantic routes. Four stretched aircraft were completed as Tudor 4s (including G-AHNN *Star Leopard*) for British South American Airways Corporation (BSAAC), configured for 32 passengers, while the company also received similar 4Bs with seating for 28 and a flight engineer's position. BSAAC flew its Tudors between London and Bermuda, but, after losing a second aircraft during unexplained circumstances in January 1949, it relegated them to carrying freight.

PERCIVAL PROCTOR

Percival developed the Proctor from the Vega Gull as a communications aircraft and radio trainer for the RAF and Admiralty, the prototype flying on 8 October 1939, from Luton Airport, Bedfordshire. Although 280 were built by Percival, the majority produced during the war were assembled by F Hills & Sons at Trafford Park, Manchester, which was responsible for 812. The 1,092 built for the RAF and Royal Navy during the war comprised 148 Proctor I communications aircraft, 99 Mk IAs for the Royal Navy, 150 Mk IIs and 437 Mk IIIs, all of which were radio trainers without dual controls, and 258 Mk IVs. Originally known as the Preceptor, the Proctor IV had a deeper and longer fuselage for four occupants (rather than three) and was used both as a trainer and communications aircraft. Post-war, Percival adapted around 200 surplus Proctors for the civil market while also developing the Proctor 5, of which 154 were produced, including four supplied to the RAF for air attachés overseas. During 1946, Percival received an order for a single Proctor floatplane from the Hudson's Bay Company of Canada. A Proctor 5 airframe was fitted with Edo floats, gaining the 'B-class marks' X1 in June 1947 for test flights by Short at Rochester, Kent. It made its public debut at the Society of British Aircraft Constructors Flying Display and Exhibition at Radlett in Hertfordshire during September 1947, before going to Canada as CF-EHF.

PLANET SATELLITE

Despite its futuristic looks and novel design concepts, the Planet Satellite was a failure. Built of magnesium-zirconium alloy, around 40 per cent lighter than aluminium, it had a monocoque structure without internal reinforced members. After securing finance for the project from a distiller, the prototype Satellite was assembled at the Robinson Redwing factory at Croydon in 1947 before being transported to Redhill. It travelled by road to Farnborough where it was displayed at the airshow held in September 1948 (as seen here), after which it was transferred to nearby Blackbushe to begin its flight test programme. In April 1949, the prototype was registered as G-ALOI. Test pilot Group Captain Hugh Joseph 'Willie' Wilson managed to 'hop' the Satellite at Blackbushe, although the landing gear collapsed returning to the runway. After repairs, another attempt to fly the Satellite was made, and while it lifted 20ft (6m) above the runway, the main keel cracked touching down. Investigation of the damage highlighted that the aircraft could not absorb the stresses of flight and needed a complete redesign, resulting in all work on the Satellite coming to an end. The fuselage of the second prototype was incorporated into the Firth FH-01/4 Atlantic helicopter in 1952, which also failed to fly.

AIRSPEED AS.57 AMBASSADOR

Two Ambassador I prototypes were ordered by the Ministry of Aircraft Production in September 1946 to meet the Brabazon Committee's Type IIA specification for a Douglas DC-3 replacement. The first, G-AGUA, made its maiden flight from Christchurch, Hampshire, on 10 July 1947. After British European Airways (BEA) selected the Ambassador in December 1947, Airspeed decided to install Bristol Centaurus engines in the second prototype, instead of the four Napier Naiads originally planned, so that the aircraft represented the configuration wanted by the airline. The second prototype was also the first with a pressurised cabin. Registered as G-AKRD, it made its maiden flight on 26 August 1948; BEA ordered 20 Ambassador 2s on 23 September. The third aircraft, G-ALFR, was built as a production prototype. BEA put the Ambassador into service as its Elizabethan class on 2 August 1951, operating them for six years. Only 23 Ambassadors were built as marketing effectively ended when de Havilland took over Airspeed in 1951. Ambassadors proved popular with passengers, and many former BEA aircraft remained in service into the late 1960s.

ARMSTRONG WHITWORTH AW.55 APOLLO

Arguably one of the most aesthetically pleasing aircraft of the early post-war period, the Apollo was designed by Armstrong Whitworth in response to Specification C.16/46, written around the Brabazon Committee's Type IIB requirement for a turboprop airliner. The prototype Apollo, VX220, later G-AIYN, flew from Baginton in Warwickshire on 10 April 1949, but was found to be unstable, requiring the addition of a fin fillet. The Armstrong Siddeley Mamba turboprops proved to be its Achilles' heel, however, as the engine fell short of its expected output, making it impossible to achieve the performance originally predicted. Although the company persevered with the Apollo, continuing performance and engine problems resulted in the development programme ending in June 1952. A second Apollo was completed and flew in December 1952, with both aircraft going to the A&AEE at Boscombe Down and the Empire Test Pilots' School.

DE HAVILLAND DH.106 COMET

By harnessing the British lead in turbojet technology, de Havilland aimed to develop an airliner with better performance than contemporary American piston-engined transports. Development of a jet airliner was authorised in February 1945 and two prototypes were ordered by the Ministry of Supply in September 1946. BOAC ordered eight in January 1947 (and soon added a ninth). On 25 July 1949, the prototype, G-5-1 (later G-ALVG), seen here, rolled out at Hatfield, Hertfordshire, with test pilot John Cunningham performing its maiden flight two days later. With its sleek looks, high speed and a pressurised cabin, the Comet was poised to become a common sight at the world's airports. The first production Comet 1 flew on 9 January 1951, and BOAC flew the inaugural jet service between London and Johannesburg, South Africa, on 2 May 1952. Two years later, after three unexplained crashes, all Comets were grounded while an investigation was undertaken. It was eventually determined that cracks caused by metal fatigue had caused the loss of two of the Comets. Although new, safe variants were developed, the Comet never fully overcame the sigma of the crashes; its chance to dominate the market had passed.

INDEX

Aircraft

People